BUS REVIEW 11

Review of 1995
Published 1996

GW00402171

In its centenary year Dennis built a record number of buses and coaches. Many of these were Darts, including unusual two-door examples for Thames Transit. They had Plaxton Pointer bodies. *Tony Wilson*

Front cover: Clydeside 2000 had suffered from under-investment when British Bus took it over, something which its new owners quickly addressed. As part of a sizeable intake of new buses at the start of 1995 the company received 10 Dennis Lances with Plaxton Verde bodies. They are the only Lances in Scotland. *John Burnett*

Back cover, upper: Q Drive took delivery of ten of these Scania L113 with Northern Counties Paladin bodywork. *Stewart J Brown*

Back cover, lower: Five Volvo Olympians with Alexander Royale bodies were added to the Finglands fleet in August to replace older double-deckers. Four, including this bus, were new. The fifth was a former demonstrator.

Contents

Introduction...3
New in the North..4
1995 Roundup 6
New for 1995 10
North East consolidation.....................................14
New in Scotland 15
Stagecoach - on the right track.........................17
Coach and Bus 95..20
New buses in London...24
Iveco launch Eurocoach 27
FirstBus - a new name in buses.........................28

Rationalisation in Sheffield................................30
Who makes what...31
More change at British Bus...............................33
A decade of Optare 36
New in the Midlands 37
New owners at Northern Counties 39
Who owns whom… 40
New in the South...42
Dennis - riding high in its centenary year.................44
1995 deliveries 46
Forward orders 48

Volvo's Environmental Concept Bus bristled with new features. The ECB is a mobile test-bed - don't expect to fin one pulling up at a bus stop near you.

First published 1996
ISBN 0 - 946265 - 23 - 2
© Bus Enthusiast Publishing Company, 1996
Typeset in Times and Helvetica
Electronic page makeup by Jeremy Scott
Printed by Pillans & Wilson, Edinburgh

Published by
Bus Enthusiast Publishing Company
5 Hallcroft Close, Ratho, Newbridge
Midlothian EH28 8SD
Bus Enthusiast is an imprint of
Arthur Southern Ltd.

Introduction

THE CHANGE OF PACE in Britain's bus industry showed no signs of slowing down in 1995. The merger of Badgerline and GRT produced a powerful new group - FirstBus. Although it remained number two (to Stagecoach) at the end of the year, there were signs that in 1996 the new group might well achieve the aspirations implicit in its name and overtake Stagecoach to become Britain's biggest bus company.

There were changes in all of the big bus groups, as consolidation continued and former NBC management buy-outs one by one sold out to the majors. Cambus and its Milton Keynes subsidiaries were bought by Stagecoach. FirstBus took over People's Provincial. British Bus bought Caldaire Holdings in Yorkshire and Maidstone & District in Kent. The latter gave the group an even more powerful presence in the area around London. By the end of the year relatively few former NBC companies remained independent - East Yorkshire, North Devon/Southern National, Wilts & Dorset and Yorkshire Traction.

Significant post-deregulation operators to lose their independence included Liverbus, taken over by MTL, and Sheffield Omnibus and Yorkshire Terrier, both bought by Yorkshire Traction. Old established independents were vanishing too, most notably A1 to Stagecoach, OK to the Go-Ahead Group and The Eden to United Auto. One municipal operation disappeared in 1995: Chesterfield Transport.

Among the manufacturers Dennis produced a record number of buses, helped by the popularity of its ubiquitous Dart, while Northern Counties was bought by Henlys, the owners of Plaxton - which suggests some product rationalisation may be in the offing. Optare launched two new single-deckers during 1995. The Mercedes-based Prisma got off to a good start - but as the market moves to low-floor buses it may well prove to be yet another stalled attempt by the German giant to sell big buses in Britain. Optare's integral Excel, a low-floor design, was more in keeping with the spirit of the times, offering low weight and good passenger access in a competitively-priced package.

And access was the big issue in 1995. Volvo weighed in with the B6LE and Dennis with the Dart SLF. The Dart SLF quickly attracted big orders and the signs are that it could soon replace the conventional Dart and render the Lance SLF redundant. Volvo's B10L, launched in 1994, won two substantial orders - from Ulsterbus and West Midlands Travel - but Volvo was hedging its accessibility bets with the announcement in the autumn of the B10BLE, an accessible version of the existing B10B which will be cheaper than the B10L. At the other end of the accessibility market, Marshall unveiled its Minibus at Coach & Bus 95. No orders had been announced by the end of the year, and it will be interesting to see just how operators react to a sub-Dart-size low-floor bus. Much will depend on its price.

One new model which bucked the low-floor trend was the US-built Spartan. It's hard not to conclude that someone in the US of A has misread the state of the British market. It might have all the right bits (Cummins engine, Allison gearbox). It might have a low selling price. But is it really a bus for the 1990s? Even in deregulated Britain? I think not.

This Review - now in its 11th year - is designed to encapsulate the main events of 1995 in a single volume. This year it incorporates for the first time a guide to the specifications of all the chassis and integrals which were on offer to UK bus and coach operators during the year.

As always, I have no hesitation in directing readers who want to know more to two main sources of information. *Buses* magazine, published monthly to ever-higher standards, offers its readers news and views of what's happening around the country. And for those who want to keep track of the real nitty gritty in changes of vehicle ownership there can be few buses or coaches which change hands in the British Isles without it being recorded by the PSV Circle, a dedicated body of enthusiasts. The information which the PSV Circle collates is available to its members in a range of comprehensive monthly new sheets.

Stewart J Brown
Framilode, 1996

The Stagecoach acquisition of Hartlepool Transport resulted in the first new buses in the town for ten years, allowing replacement of some of the Bristol RE fleet, by then over twenty years old. *John Burnett*

New in the North

Harrogate & District bought new buses for its Leeds to Ripon service. These were five Volvo B10Bs with Alexander Strider bodies, which carried appropriate route branding. Alexander-bodied Volvo B6s were also added to the Harrogate & District fleet in 1995.

East Yorkshire opted for Palatine II bodies from Northern Counties for six standard-wheelbase Volvo Olympians delivered in the autumn. They were accompanied by 14 long-wheelbase versions with Alexander Royale bodies. *Michael Fowler*

The Hartlepool Transport fleet, acquired by Stagecoach at the end of 1994, was badly in need of modernisation. This was started in 1995 with the delivery of new Volvo B10Ms with Northern Counties bodies. *Steve Warburton*

Smart additions to the Mainline fleet were 11 Volvo B6LE low-floor midibuses with Wright Crusader bodywork. They followed an earlier batch of conventional B6 models with Plaxton Pointer bodies. *Michael Fowler*

CMT took delivery of its first new buses in 1995. Wright-bodied Volvo B10Bs joined the fleet in the spring and were followed by Dennis Darts with Northern Counties bodies towards the end of the year. The fleet had previously been made up of Mark 1 Leyland Nationals. This is one of four B10Bs with Wright Endurance bodywork.

The Volvo B10L with Alexander Ultra body appeared in just three British fleets in 1995 - Fife Scottish, Northampton Transport and Timeline. The last-named took six for operation on services in the Bolton and Bury areas.

1995 Roundup

A month-by-month summary of events in the bus and coach industry in 1995.

January

• New British Bus subsidiary Londonlinks Buses takes over London & Country's operations in Croydon, Walworth and Dunton Green, with a fleet of 162 vehicles.

• The Cowie Group buys South London Transport, bringing to a close the privatisation of London Buses' bus-operating subsidiaries.

• GM Buses North announces withdrawal of its Southport services. MTL Manchester cuts back in Manchester. GM Buses North also pulls out of Liverpool, but GM Buses South expands its operations in the city.

• British Bus subsidiary North Western launches local services in Warrington under the Warrington Goldlines name, running in competition with Warrington Borough Transport.

• Brents Travel of Watford buys Scorpio Travel of Gosport.

• Britain's first commercially-operated guided busway opens at Kesgrave, near Ipswich. It is served by Eastern Counties Superoute 66, using modified Dennis Darts equipped with lateral guidewheels.

• Iveco announced that it is launching a full-size bus in the UK, the EuroRider. It will be bodied by Marshall. It also has plans to market the 7m-long DownTown midibus which has a low - 330mm - floor. A further low-floor design, originally developed jointly with Kassbohrer, is on the cards for the UK market in 1996.

• Stagecoach takes over A1 of Ardrossan (67 buses).

• The Department of Transport announces that from 1 January 1996 coaches weighing more than 7.5 tonnes will be banned from the outside lane of motorways with three or more lanes.

February

• A £5 million refurbishment of Glasgow's Buchanan bus station is completed. Opened in 1977, it is the biggest bus station in Scotland. It handles 30,000 passengers and 1,400 buses daily.

• Golden Coaches closes and its routes are taken over by Cardiff Bus.

• Citibus Tours of Manchester (54 vehicles), owned by Lynton Travel, is sold to GM Buses North.

• Cacciamali of Italy is to import small buses to the UK through Robin Hood Vehicle Industries. The aim is to move to local UK assembly with a target output of 175 a year. R&I Coaches express an interest in ordering 18 Autobus Urbano TCN890 8.9m midibuses for operation in London.

• The takeover of Kassbohrer by Mercedes-Benz gets EU approval. Between them the two companies claim a 28 per cent share of the European bus and coach market. The new combined organisation is known as Evobus. Kassbohrer UK announces that it has orders for 24 Setras for 1995 delivery.

• Omni relaunch three-axle minibus, which offers 21 seats instead of the 16 of the original two-axle model. The first goes to Whippet of Fenstanton

• Wilts & Dorset buys Tourist Coaches of Figheldean (15 vehicles).

• Cambus subsidiaries Buckinghamshire Road Car and Milton Keynes City Bus are merged, with Road Car taking-over 40 Mercedes minibuses from City Bus. Both fleetnames are retained.

March

• British Bus buys Caldaire Holdings which operates 400 vehicles. This takes the British Bus fleet to 5,000, making it number two after Stagecoach.

• EYMS adopts a new crimson and cream livery, replacing the previous red and grey introduced in 1986.

• Warrington Borough Transport launches new services from Warrington to Wigan, Widnes and Skelmersdale in response to North Western's attack on the company's Warrington local routes.

• First UK Neoplan N4009s are delivered to MTL. The N4009 is a low-floor midi, 9m long and 2.5m wide. It has a 155bhp MAN D0824LOH engine and a Voith Midimat four-speed automatic gearbox with integral retarder. Prices start at £105,000.

• Go-Ahead Group acquires OK Motor Services, which runs 200 buses. The takeover is referred to the MMC.

• Dennis announce low-floor Dart SLF chassis.

• The Greater Manchester PTE announces plans to fund 29 low-floor buses for Stagecoach Ribble (five), GM Buses North (five), Bullocks (four), Starline (five), Stuarts (four) and Timeline (six).

• Local bus services are started in Motherwell by Coakley of New Stevenston, using former Scottish Bus Group Seddons.

April

• Rhondda Buses takes over Parfitt's, running 47 buses.

• National Express takes over the competing Yorkshire Express operation which was started in the autumn of 1993 and ran from Bradford and Leeds to London.

• Delta Arrowline is set up by a Mansfield taxi company, running services to Nottingham in competition with Trent. Its fleet is made up mainly of second-hand minibuses.

• Toppings of Liverpool (20 vehicles) closes. Its newest buses - four Leyland Lynxes - had been sold to PMT when the company pulled out of bus operation at the end of 1994.

• The use of school bus signs becomes compulsory on buses carrying children to or from school.

• D Coaches buys the 27-vehicle Glantawe Coaches business. D Coaches is based in Morriston; Glantawe in Pontardawe. The Glantawe name will be retained. The takeover boosts the D Coaches fleet to 90 vehicles.

• GM Buses North takes over the services - but not the vehicles - of Dalybus of Eccles.

• Ensign Bus takes over the operation of the Hop on-Hop off London tourist service.

• British Bus buys Maidstone & District.

• WMT merges with National Express.

• MTL Trust Holdings takes over Liverbus and the associated London Suburban operations. Liverbus runs 43 buses in Liverpool and started in January 1990. London Suburban has 51 buses in north London and commenced operating in September 1993.

• DSB Sales, the Midlands-based coach dealer, unveils the MarcoPolo Explorer body for the Dennis Javelin at the Brighton coach rally. Designed in Brazil, it is built in Portugal.

May

• Badgerline and GRT merge. The new group is called FirstBus and has 5,600 vehicles. It is second in size to Stagecoach.

• MTL and GM Buses North end head-on competition in Liverpool and Manchester as each withdraws from the other's operating area. The bus war between the two had been triggered by MTL launching services in Manchester in October 1993. As part of the deal GMBN acquires 30 vehicles from MTL - 21 Nationals and nine Bolton Coachways minibuses.

• EYMS buys Hart Coaches of Stockton (11 vehicles). The operation is renamed Teesside Coach Travel.

• K-Line launches local services in Wakefield using Leyland Nationals.

• Ten people die when a Jonckheere-bodied Volvo B10M operated by Laguna of Bournemouth leaves the M4 near the Severn Bridge and rolls down an embankment.

• Henlys Group and Volvo buy Canadian manufacturer Prevost. The company builds 500 vehicles a year. Volvo and Plaxton plan to export B12Ts to North America.

• Transit Holdings wins contracts to run 113 Mercedes 811D minibuses in Queensland. The services will be operated by Transit Australia.

• Volvo launches B10M SE, which offers improved luggage accommodation.

• Luton & District becomes LDT, trading as The Shires and with a new livery and fleet names.

• Stagecoach Holdings acquires an interest in the 150-vehicle Rodoviaria de Lisboa operation, serving Lisbon, Cascais, Estoril and Sintra.

• Walter Alexander and Hong Kong bus operator KMB form Dragon Pioneer International to manufacture buses in China.

• The Shires takes over the 24-vehicle bus operation of Buffalo Travel of Flitwick.

• White Rose of Castleford abandons its Routemaster operation in Leeds. It had started in December 1994.

• Star Line of Knutsford is sold to British Bus. It ran 45 vehicles. The takeover is referred to the MMC.

• Stagecoach is instructed by the MMC to sell its 20 per cent shareholding in SB Holdings.

• Buckinghamshire Road Car is renamed MK Metro - but with no change of identity on the vehicles other than the legal lettering.

June

• The Le Shuttle coach-carrying service through the Channel Tunnel is officially launched after a few months of trial operation.

• Ashford Luxury Coaches takes over Windsorian Coaches.

• Pattersons Coaches gives up its local bus services in Birmingham.

• Q Drive takes over Limebourne Travel of London (24 coaches).

• City Buslines of Birmingham ceases operations. It had started in November 1993 and ran 15 Leyland Nationals.

• Lothian Region Transport adopts new Airline branding for its service to Edinburgh airport.

• Mainline announces that it intends to bid to operate bus services under franchise in Adelaide.

• Express Travel ends its competition with National Express and reverts to its role as a supplier of coaches for the National Express network. It had been running competing services since September 1994.

• The first MAN 18.370 to be fitted with Caetano Algarve II body is delivered to Wide Horizon Coaches of Hinckley. The 18.370 had previously only been available in the UK with Berkhof bodywork.

• GM Buses North absorbs the Citibus operation which it had acquired in February from Lynton Travel.

• Budget Busways introduces services in the Colchester area using Leyland Nationals.

July

• South Lancs Transport launches services in Chester using second-hand minibuses.

• Fire at Yorkshire Rider's Torre Road garage in Leeds destroys 13 double-deck buses. Arson is suspected.

• Van Hool introduce a short Eos, the Eos 80. It is 9.5m long and has a 290bhp Mercedes OM401LA engine. Maximum capacity is 39 seats.

• MTL Manchester operations cease, as do the Birkenhead & District operations of GM Buses South.

• East Lancs announces that it will start building bodies using the Alusuisse system of aluminium extrusions. This was first used in the UK by Wright of Ballymena, and then by Optare.

• The Shires takes over the bus operations of Motts of Aylesbury, started in 1991 under the Yellow Buses name (17 vehicles). Motts retains its coach business.

• Midland Bluebird buys Kings of Dunblane, a long-established coach operator.

• Eight people are killed when a Duple-bodied DAF belonging to Lewis Coaches of Aberdare overturns at a roundabout on the A40 at Raglan.

• Britain's first open-top minibus, a 16-seat B-registered Transit, goes into service with M-Travel of Ventnor on the Isle of Wight.

• Chiltern European goes into voluntary liquidation. The company ran 10 coaches and had previously been part of Luton & District.

• TBP launches a low-floor minibus based on the Peugeot Boxer. It has two rear axles and a stepped roof line over the raised rear portion of the body.

August

• The former Caldaire companies Selby & District, West Riding and Yorkshire Woollen adopt simplified liveries which do away with the upswept band of colour towards the fronts of buses.

• Volvo unveils its ECB (Environmental Concept Bus) at an exhibition in Bruges.

• Ogdens of St Helens gives up bus operation. Its services are taken over by MTL and by another St Helens independent, Hatton.

• Volvo starts building B10M chassis at its Irvine plant. Irvine already builds the Olympian and the B6.

Routemaster operation in Hull came to an end in 1995. However the old-style dark blue East Yorkshire livery has survived and is now carried by a small number of Leyland Olympians.
Michael Fowler

• Scania announce new East Lancs-bodied Cityzen double-decker.

• The Mayflower group buys Walter Alexander.

• A prototype 11m lowfloor chassis for British Bus is built by Kirn Vehicle Engineering, a West Yorkshire design consultancy. It is powered by a Cummins C-series engine and has an Allison MT647 gearbox. It is to be bodied by East Lancs and is intended for operation by North Western.

• Budget Busways of Colchester closes after seven weeks.

• Stagecoach buys Chesterfield Transport. Whites of Calver, a Chesterfield subsidiary, is closed. The takeover is referred to the MMC.

• Plaxton announce that the Premiere body will be available on the DAF SB3000WS rear-engined chassis for 1996. It had previously been offered only on Dennis and Volvo chassis.

• Autobus Classique of Rotherham launches its Nouvelle on Mercedes 814D chassis. Prices start at £68,000. High-spec models are called the Exceutif and the Etoile.

• East Yorkshire withdraws its Routemasters. They had been running in Hull since 1988.

September

• Delta of Kirkby in Ashfield expands its Nottingham area services with the acquisition of no fewer than 37 second-hand buses including nine double-deckers - ex Kelvin Central Dominators.

• WM Travel sells Westlink to London United (131 buses).

• Bere Regis & District closes after selling the bulk of its operations to Cawlett in March 1994.

• The first phase of the Leeds guided busway opens, on the A61. It is used by Alexander-bodied Scania N113 Superbuses operated by Leeds City Link (Yorkshire Rider as was).

• Glossopdale Bus Company buys Tame Valley of Stalybridge.

October

• FirstBus subsidiary Brewer takes over the coach operations of Cardiff City Transport (four vehicles), along with its Vale Busline operations, based on the former Golden Coaches operations acquired in February.

• Buscraft of Birkenhead launches its Impala body on the Mercedes-Benz 814L chassis. The body has an entrance ahead of the front axle. The complete coach sells for £71,500.

• FirstBus buys Provincial (155 buses).

• MTL London Northern takes control of the 50-strong London Suburban fleet, which is to be repainted red.

• The 2,000th MetroRider is delivered to Trent.

• Jonckheere unveil new Mistral 50 coach body - but it will not be available until 1997. The right-hand-drive prototype is in the livery of Clarkes of London.

• Wright announce a new full-size low-floor body, the Liberator, on Volvo B10L chassis. Production is to start in 1996. The company also plans to extend its factory to cope with increasing orders.

• MAN and Marshall are to produce an 11.8m low-floor bus for the UK market, based on MAN's NL222FR chassis. It will be launched in mid-1996.

• The Volvo B12.600, built by Drogmoller, Volvo's German subsidiary, is voted European Coach of the Year 1996.

• Largs bus station is closed. It was a simple pre-war structure alongside the railway station (itself demolished by a runaway train in the summer) which dated back to the days of Young's Bus Service.

• Berkhof launches the Axial, to replace the Excellence 1000 range.

• Glossopdale Bus Company introduces a route in South West Scotland, trading as the Galloway Bus Company.

• Van Hool announce the T9 range, to replace the existing T8 models.

• MTL Trust Holdings buys R&I, which runs 39 buses and 25 coaches. The coach operation is to be rebranded as Sightseers London.

• Highland Country Buses is formed by Rapsons, owners of Highland Scottish, to take over the Highland Scottish operations outside Inverness. Its initial fleet comprises 66 buses and coaches 41 of which date from the late 1970s. Highland Scottish is left with 40 vehicles.

November

• Badgerline is re-united with Bristol City Line - but both companies retain their individual identities.

• Dennis announce three-axle Javelin chassis for operation in New Zealand and a two-axle high-frame option for 3.5m-high bodywork, such as the Neoplan Transliner.

• Barnsley & District, part of Yorkshire Traction, takes over the bus operations of Globe of Barnsley.

• Ambermile launches services in Barnsley with a fleet of a dozen Mark 1 Leyland Nationals. They are competing with Yorkshire Traction.

December

• Stagecoach buys Cambus Holdings, with 370 vehicles.

• Geldard Coaches introduces a bus service between Headingley and Leeds using five Leyland Nationals running under the Bigfoot name.

• FirstBus takes over the 20 per cent share in Mainline which had previously been held by Stagecoach.

• Country Lion of Northampton takes over the coach operations of Brittains (eight vehicles).

• Stagecoach is the successful bidder for the South West Trains franchise in the first round of rail privatisation.

• Scottish Citylink takes over Gaelicbus of Ballachulish (18 vehicles).

• The Scottish Traffic Commissioner bans Coakley of New Stevenston from running local bus services after complaints about operating irregularities. Services had been started in the Motherwell area in March.

Volvo first with low-floor midi

VOLVO is still Britain's biggest bus and coach supplier, even if Dennis is running neck and neck in the race to lead in bus sales. One race which Volvo did win was the low-floor midi stakes. It unveiled its low-floor B6, the B6LE (Low Entry), in April, with an attractive body - the Crusader - by Wright of Ballymena.

The B6LE is a revision of the original B6, launched in 1991, and both models are built in Britain, at Volvo's Irvine bus and truck plant. Power for the B6LE comes from Volvo's 5.48-litre TD63E engine, a high-volume unit found in the FL6 truck range. In trucks it runs at up to 250bhp, but for the B6LE a more modest 180 horses are deemed adequate. A 210bhp option is offered. A ZF 4HP500 four-speed torque-converter gearbox is fitted.

The B6LE has air suspension with a kneeling facility, a carry over from the original model. This reduces the entrance step height from 320mm to 240mm. Like the Dennis Dart, it runs on 19.5in wheels.

Volvo launched the original B6 with three options on length - 8.5m, 9m and 9.9m. Lack of interest in short buses has seen the new B6LE appear in two lengths - 9.8m and 10.6m. The Wright-bodied demonstrator which launched the B6LE was followed up by a vehicle in London General livery. This was exhibited at the UITP show in Paris in the summer, and entered trial service with London General in the autumn. Back in 1992 London General did in fact order a batch of B6s, but switched the order to Dennis when Volvo were unable to meet tight delivery schedules. The Wright-bodied B6LE is the first B6 of any description for a former London Buses subsidiary.

The Wright Crusader body on the 10.6m B6LE can carry up to 36 seated and 18 standing passengers.

At Coach & Bus 95 there were two B6LEs on show. On the

Volvo's low-floor B6LE was launched in the spring. All of those which entered service in 1995 had Wright Crusader bodies. The launch vehicle is seen on demonstration in Scunthorpe. *Michael Fowler*

Wright stand there was a 37-seater for GM Buses North, billed as a "Very Low Floor" bus, to distinguish it from the Wright-bodied B10Bs delivered earlier in the year which were somewhat confusingly described by GMBN as low floor buses. The other B6LE was a demonstrator with Plaxton's revised Pointer body. The latter weighed 7732kg - over a tonne heavier than a Dart alongside - while the GM Buses North vehicle weighed 8360kg. If that seems a lot for a midibus - which it is alongside the Dart or even against Optare's 7940kg Excel - pause to ponder on how those vehicles which were midibuses have grown. The fact is that 10.6m B6LE is the same length as a short Leyland National 2...

Deliveries of B6LEs in 1995 were to Mainline in Sheffield, which took nine (with another two due at the start of 1996), and Ralphs Coaches at Heathrow which got two for a hotel contract. All of these had Wright bodies. At the launch of the B6LE in April Volvo was claiming that there were over 550 B6s in service with bus operators in the UK.

New access bus from Scania

SCANIA'S low-floor MaxCi, based on the N113 and bodied by East Lancs, was far from being an instant success. Launched at Coach & Bus 93, sales were sluggish. It suffered from, among other things, an unfortunate layout at the rear where there were all the signs of a compromise design with a multiplicity of floor levels over the rear axle and engine. And it didn't look very good either.

The solution to these problems appeared in March, when Scania unveiled the Axcess-ultralow, based on the low-frame L113CRL chassis and bodied by Wright of Ballymena. The L113CRL uses a drop-beam Scania front axle with air suspension. Like all new low-floor models the front suspension can be lowered, in this case to give a step height of 200mm.

The L113 differs from the more expensive N113 in its use of an in-line inclined engine. rather than a transverse installation. It's the same Scania DSC11 unit, rated at 234bhp to meet current Euro 1 emission legislation, or 265bhp to meet the Euro 2 limits from autumn 1996. A ZF 4HP500 automatic gearbox is fitted.

The Wright body uses the proven Alusuisse system and in standard layout is a 47-seater with space for 26 standees. This is claimed to be the highest seating capacity of any low-floor design on offer in the UK. Take out four seats and you can increase the number of standees to 31, to give a maximum carrying capacity of 74. The floor is flat and unobstructed until the rear axle.

The Axcess-ultralow - not the catchiest name in the business - quickly won orders from Rider York, which called for 20 for use on park-and-ride services, and British Bus, which put 10 into its Kentish Bus fleet. Smaller numbers were delivered to Nottingham City Transport and Bullock of Cheadle. And it seems fair to suggest that with its arrival, we won't be seeing any more East Lancs-bodied MaxCi buses.

Spartan by name - and by nature?

THE SPARTANS were ancient Greeks whose legacy to the English language is the adjective which means, according to Collins Concise English Dictionary, "very strict or austere". Would you call your bus a Spartan? The Americans would, and the first for a British operator was bodied by East Lancs and unveiled, as the Opus 2, at Coach & Bus 95. Whatever happened to Opus 1, you

The Spartan was used by East Lancs to herald the company's adoption of the Alusuisse system of construction, already in use (with rather more flair) by Wright and Optare. Named the Opus 2, it raises the question: Whatever happened to Opus 1? *Stewart J Brown*

might well ask.

The Spartan features a straightforward chassis with a rear-mounted Cummins B-series engine rated at either 210bhp or 230bhp, Allison four-speed gearbox, Eaton axle and air suspension. UK Spartans will have 24 volt electrics - but that is actually an option in the model's home market where a 12 volt system is standard.

The conservative Spartan chassis was in fact covered by a body which was more interesting than it first appeared, being the first East Lancs body to be built using the Alusuisse system. East Lancs became in 1995 the third UK builder to gain access to the Alusuisse method of construction (following Wright and Optare) and the Opus 2 was the first fruits of this. A new Alusuisse midibus body is on the drawing board for 1996 and the double-deck Cityzen, initially built using a conventional aluminium frame, has been designed so that it, too, can be produced using Alusuisse extrusions.

Spartan is the second US builder to target the UK bus market and the question has to be asked whether it will be any more successful than the first, Blue Bird, which appeared in 1992 and has notched up very few sales in the intervening period. The only significant Blue Bird delivery in Britain in 1995 was a batch of eight for West Sussex county council's school bus fleet. And that's a figure the Spartan might just be struggling to match.

The launch vehicle was for Yorkshire Traction.

Dart goes low-floor

THE DENNIS DART has been a runaway success for a company which 10 years ago was overshadowed by giants such as Leyland and Volvo. By the end of 1995 over 3,000 had been sold since the model was first shown at the 1988 Motor Show with bodywork by Duple, at that time a sister company of Dennis in the Hestair group. Duple is no more, although its Dartline body concept lives on at Marshall of Cambridge. But Dennis has gone from strength to strength.

With growing interest in accessible low-floor buses, it was only a matter of time before Dennis adapted the principles which it had applied to the Lance SLF in 1993, to produce a Dart equivalent. This it did in 1995, and the Dart SLF was unveiled at Coach & Bus 95. The letters indicate Super Low Floor.

The Dart SLF carries over the proven Cummins/Allison driveline of the original model, but with the inclusion of a Telma retarder as standard. Early Darts often came in for criticism on brake lining wear and the Telma had in fact been offered as an option in recent years. The 5.9-litre Cummins B-series is offered in Euro 2 guise, which means that it meets tighter new emission controls which come into effect in October 1996. It is rated at 130bhp on the two shorter models (9m and 10m), and at 145bhp in the 10.5m Super Dart - which looks set to be the most popular variant. The gearbox is the four-speed AT545 automatic.

The original Dart - which continues in production (it's slightly cheaper) - used taper leaf springs. The Dart SLF has air suspension with a front kneeling facility, which allows the entrance step to be lowered by 80mm, from 325mm to just 245mm. Both types of Dart run on low-profile tyres fitted to 19.5in wheels.

The low front frame of the Dart SLF means that there is a flat floor until just ahead of the rear axle, where two steps lead to the raised rear section. The majority of passengers can be accommodated in the low front section.

The Dennis Dart SLF has a low floor to provide easy access. The first examples were bodied by Plaxton with a revised Pointer body which is 100mm wider than the original.

The first examples have all been bodied by Plaxton, who have bodied around half of Dennis's production of Darts, but the Dart SLF chassis will be available to any builder who bodied the original model. The new-generation Pointer body might not look much different, but it is wider, 2.4m against 2.3m, and under the skin uses some of the aluminium sections of Plaxton's full-size Verde.

There were three Plaxton-bodied Dart SLFs at Coach & Bus 95. On the Dennis stand there was a two-door 27-seater in CentreWest colours which, on a show vehicle,

doesn't necessarily mean that it's going to CentreWest. Time will tell. It was displayed alongside a 41-seat single-door demonstrator. Plaxton showed a 37-seater for FirstBus subsidiary Thamesway, the first of 10 similar buses.

The Thamesway vehicle was exhibited by Plaxton alongside the rival B6LE. The Volvo had a more lavish interior specification but that alone could not account for the 20 per cent weight difference - 7732kg for the B6LE against 6464kg for the Dart SLF. Sales of the original Dart have romped way ahead of those of the B6. Initial indications are that the same will happen with the Dart SLF versus the B6LE.

No Dart SLFs entered service in 1995 but early orders for 1996 came from Brighton Transport, Q Drive Buses and British Bus.

Optare set to excel

OPTARE can be relied upon to produce new vehicles with style. The new Excel, unveiled at Coach & Bus 95, was no exception. Yet it broke with the traditional Optare look as first seen on the Delta in 1988, so perhaps seven years on it was time to ring the changes.

The Excel marks a departure for Optare in that it is a large integral. Previously the only integral built by the Leeds company was the MetroRider, a design inherited from MCW. All other current Optare products are built on other makers' chassis - DAF, Dennis, MAN and Mercedes-Benz - and use Alusuisse aluminium extrusions. The integral Excel is steel-framed, at a time when most other builders of buses in this class offer aluminium-built bodies.

At its launch Optare was promising the Excel in four lengths, from a 9.3m midi-class bus, through 10m and 10.7m variants (all competing with the Dart SLF and B6LE) to a full-size 11.4m bus, which pretty well takes it into the same market segment as the Lance SLF, Volvo B10L and Scania Axcess-ultralow. It stands apart from the B6LE and Dart SLF in being a full 2.5m wide, rather than 2.4m. Seating will range from 32 to 44.

It uses the same 5.9-litre Cummins B-series engine as Dennis's Dart range, but rated at 160bhp. A MAN engine is to be available in left-hand drive export models. The Excel also has an Allison gearbox, but not the AT545. Optare has instead specified the B300R World Series electronically-controlled automatic, which has an integral retarder. A Rockwell rear axle is fitted, with MAN providing the front axle. Air suspension is, of course, standard and, as on all low-floor buses, comes with a kneeling ability which lowers the entry step from 320mm to 250mm. The Excel has full-size 22.5in wheels, a reflection of its role as a full-size bus as well as a midi.

The Optare Excel marks a departure from Optare's previous policy of building full-size bus bodies on separate chassis. It is of integral construction, following the success of the company's smaller integral MetroRider. *Stewart J Brown*

Optare's Mercedes

THERE'S ONE THING which the Mercedes-Benz O405 is definitely not, and that's new. It's been around since the mid-1980s, and Mercedes have made efforts to sell it in the UK, with but limited success. Its last attempt was in 1992, with the unveiling of an O405 with Alexander PS-type body. This was marketed as the Cityranger and GRT ordered 20, although when they arrived in 1993 they had bodywork by Wright rather than by Alexander. One articulated O405G was also built for GRT, entering service at the end of 1992. It did have an Alexander body.

Then all went quiet. However new life was breathed into the moribund O405 in March, when Optare unveiled its Prisma, marrying the Leeds company's Alusuisse structure to the Mannheim-built underframe. The result, undeniably a fine vehicle, lacks Optare's usual styling flair because it uses the standard Mercedes front end structure and windscreens. The Prisma might be more expensive than a Delta, but it doesn't look it.

The O405 has a space frame chassis with, unusually in the turbocharged 1990s, a naturally-aspirated engine. This is a Mercedes OM447H six-cylinder 12-litre unit, rated at 213bhp and driving through a ZF 4HP500 automatic gearbox.

Sales of Prismas got off to a healthy start with orders from North East Bus for 25 and from GRT Bus Group for 30 - ten each for Eastern Scottish in Edinburgh, Grampian Transport in Aberdeen and Leicester Citybus. The GRT order pre-dated the formation of FirstBus, so whether the new combine will be buying further buses of this type remains to be seen. Three other Prismas found homes in 1995, one going to a small Herefordshire operator - Sargeants of Kington - and two to Rhondda.

New Minibus from Marshall

Marshall's low-floor Minibus features a four-cylinder Cummins engine.
Stewart J Brown

MARSHALL has had some success in selling small buses, most notably with the order which it won for 120 bodies on Dennis Dart chassis for the Go-Ahead Group. That body is the successor to the original body offered on the Dart, the Duple Dartline, launched at a time when both Duple and Dennis were sister companies in the Hestair group.

At Coach & Bus 95 Marshall launched a new integral, somewhat prosaically named the Minibus. It's a smartly-styled low-floor 8.5m model designed to offer up to 30 seats. The Minibus has a stainless steel frame and a rear-mounted 3.9-litre Cummins B-series four-cylinder engine rated at 135bhp. A four-cylinder Perkins Phaser is offered as an option. An Allison automatic gearbox is fitted. The Minibus has disc brakes all round, but with air-hydraulic operation, rather than full air.

On the launch vehicle Marshall had imaginatively mounted two rearward facing child seats, complete with harnesses. A nice idea, although it's hard to see it catching on. Most parents surely prefer to have small children travelling beside them -and many small children can become unbearably vocal if separated from their parents in a strange environment. A ramp is incorporated in the front step to ease access for wheelchairs.

For saloon heating Marshall has revived an idea first seen on the Leyland National, with warm air being blown down the body side from roof level. This is designed to prevent the windows misting up.

At first glance the Marshall Minibus might seem to be a competitor for the Dennis Dart. But the Dart (and the Volvo B6) have grown. The shortest Dart SLF is 9m, and it seems likely that most Dart SLFs will in fact be longer. Which then has Marshall aiming at the Mercedes-Benz market, where an 811D typically carries 33-seat bodywork with a narrow three-step entrance.

There can be no question that the Marshall Minibus offers a more attractive travelling environment than any small vehicle based on a light truck chassis. But can it really compete on price with high-volume chassis from Mercedes and, to a lesser extent, Iveco? Or even with Optare's integral MetroRider which offers the sophistication of Cummins' bigger six-cylinder B-series unit? Orders placed in 1996 will show.

North East consolidation

BIG CHANGES IN the ownership of buses in the north-east of England in 1994 were continued in 1995. In 1994 Stagecoach was the main player, but in 1995 it was the Go-Ahead Group which was making the running.

The Go-Ahead Group ranks as joint number five in bus-ownership in Britain, with around 1,700 buses putting it alongside MTL but behind the big three - Stagecoach, FirstBus and British Bus, and also behind West Midlands Travel. It is the inheritor of the Northern General operations in Tyne & Wear and County Durham, bought from NBC by the company's management back in 1987. Expansion in the south - buying City of Oxford, Brighton & Hove and London Central - meant that by the start of 1995 over half of the Go-Ahead Group's fleet - then around 1,500-strong - was based in the south. But not for long. The balance swung north again with the takeover in March of OK Motor Services of Bishop Auckland, an old-established and well-respected independent.

OK's roots - and some of its routes - could be traced back to the days before the 1930 Road Traffic Act and the regulation of bus services in Britain. Over the years the company had bought a mixture of new and used buses, making for an interesting fleet which was always well turned out. Deregulation of Britain's buses in 1986 saw the company embark on a course of rapid expansion. Its fleet was around the 70 mark in 1986. When the Go-Ahead Group took over it had risen to 200.

Leylands figured strongly, with 48 Atlanteans and 56 Leopards. There were other types too, Olympians and Tigers, plus a unique rear-engined Tiger. This had been built in the mid-1980s for demonstration in Bangkok and had a two-door ECW body. Its role as a demonstrator was never fulfilled and after a brief period with the Leyland DAF football club in the early 1990s it was bought by OK and rebuilt for use as a bus, which involved new seats, removal of the

centre door and replacement of the full-depth sliding windows. It entered OK service in the early part of 1995.

Over the 18 months or so prior to selling out to the Go-Ahead Group, OK had taken significant numbers of new buses into its fleet - 33 Volvo B6s, five B10Bs, and nine Mercedes-Benz 709Ds. Most of these had Alexander bodies. Under Go-Ahead ownership OK quickly assumed control of Go-Ahead's Low Fell operation and one of the first signs of this was the transfer to Low Fell of an OK B10B, repainted in Low Fell blue livery but applied in OK style.

While the OK operation was easily the Go-Ahead Group's most important acquisition in 1995, it wasn't the only one. At the start of the year it took over the operations of Diamond of Stanley. Diamond, which had been serving Stanley since the 1920s, had originally been a co-operative. The fleet when Go-Ahead took over comprised six buses, all bought new - two Y-series Bedfords, three Dennis Javelins and a Dart. In June, Go-Ahead took over Armstrong of Ebchester which ran 14 vehicles.

Other changes in the Go-Ahead empire saw the abandonment of the Tyne Rider identity, adopted at the end of 1994 but discontinued in June. Tyne Rider branding, with a blue and green livery, had been carried by five Metrobuses.

In Sunderland, W H Jolly of South Hylton gave up operation in June. The fleet comprised eight Duple-bodied Bedfords, five buses and three coaches, all bought new between 1977 and 1981. The Jolly business had been started in 1922. The company's service was taken over by Busways.

Another old-established name, The Eden, sold out in October to United Auto, part of the West Midlands Travel group. The Eden's history could be traced back to the 1920s and when United took over the fleet stood at 17 buses including eight Leopards and five Volvo-engined Nationals which had been introduced to the fleet in 1993. The Eden was based in West Auckland.

Further south, Stagecoach's Cleveland Transit took over the bus operations of Delta Coaches of Stockton in July. In return Delta acquired the 14-vehicle Cleveland Coaches operations. Delta's fleet had consisted of Bristol REs which were promptly sold. Delta had been running local services since 1986.

In February the final chapter was written in the saga which led to the closure of Darlington Transport in 1994, following aggressive competition from Stagecoach. The 29 vehicles which it owned were disposed of by auction.

OK had invested in new buses, like this long wheelbase Olympian/Northern Counties. *John Burnett*

New in Scotland

AA Buses is the only survivor of Ayrshire's old-established independent bus operators following the takeover at the start of 1995 of A1 by Stagecoach - who later in the year also acquired the commercial services of Clyde Coast. A number of new buses joined the AA fleet in 1995, including a trio of Dennis Darts with Northern Counties bodies. *Michael Fowler*

Strathtay Scottish, part of the Yorkshire Traction group, put two new Volvo Olympians into service. They had lowheight bodies by Northern Counties. *Billy Nicol*

SMT used a batch of ten Optare Prisma-bodied Mercedes-Benz O405 to operate the busy Edinburgh – West Lothian routes branded as Diamond Services. *John Burnett*

Scanias figured strongly in the Clydeside 2000 fleet renewal. This is a low-floor MaxCi with East Lancs body. *Stewart J Brown*

Four new Volvo Olympian double-deckers were bought by Strathclyde Buses, two with Northern Counties Palatine II bodywork (upper) and two with Alexander Royale bodies (lower). After six months in service they were transferred to the KCB Network fleet, but not before Strathclyde placed an order for 150 Olympians with Alexander bodies. *Stewart J Brown*

Stagecoach - on the right track

IN SOME WAYS 1995 was a deceptively quiet year for Stagecoach. It took delivery of large numbers of new buses. It signalled its second venture into rail services. It made a few acquisitions. But above all it kept brushing up against the Monopolies and Mergers Commission. Whatever Stagecoach does, it seems sure to interest the MMC.

In January the MMC launched an investigation into Stagecoach's 20 per cent stake in SB Holdings which controls Strathclyde Buses, Kelvin Central and GCT. It didn't like what it found, although by the end of the year Stagecoach still had its shareholding. The MMC wasn't too keen on another Stagecoach acquisition - A1 of Ardrossan - and that too came under the microscope.

The disappearance of A1, the Ayrshire co-operative which for decades has been a magnet for bus enthusiast, was a strong reminder that nothing is sacred in this age of change. A1 ran 67 buses and many of these were extremely old. Stagecoach quickly drafted in more modern vehicles from elsewhere in its empire, including 14 Bristol VRTs and 13 ex-London Buses Titans, which entered service in red. A1 has, of course, a long history of running ex-London buses and in the late 1950s and early 1960s had a sizeable fleet of RTs and RTLs.

A1's newest buses - mainly Olympians - were promptly repainted in corporate Stagecoach white, but older types were withdrawn as new vehicles arrived. These included 21 Alexander-bodied Volvo Olympians, the biggest single influx of new buses in A1's history - and the kind of investment which Stagecoach critics are quick to ignore.

A1 also received a few Alexander-bodied B10Ms, some of which received Coastlink 535 route branding - white with two green stripes. This was an undisguised

Stagecoach caused a stir in October with the announcement that it had placed an order for 10 Volvo B10Ms with articulated Plaxton Premiere bodies. They will be the first articulated coaches built in Britain.

attack on the Coastline 585 service operated by Ashton Coaches of Port Glasgow, whose livery was also white and green. The competing Coastlink service was run jointly by A1, Clyde Coast, Dodds Coaches and Clydeside Buses and it prompted court action by Ashton Coaches who succeeded in having the newcomers forced to rebrand their service with a new name - Clydecoaster - and a new livery using red stripes in place of green. The commercial services

Under Stagecoach ownership Kingston-upon-Hull City Transport received new Volvo B10Bs with Northern Counties Paladin bodies. These were delivered in the blue, yellow and white KHCT livery which had been introduced following the takeover of KHCT by Cleveland Transit in 1993. *Michael Fowler*

operated by Clyde Coast were taken over by Stagecoach in the summer.

There were administrative changes in the north east of England. Control of the group's controversial Darlington operations was transferred from Busways to Cleveland Transit, which was also responsible for operations in Hartlepool and Hull. Do the worthy citizens of Hull notice that what they might still see as the Corporation's buses actually carry an address in Stockton on the side? Cleveland Transit took over the bus operations of Delta Coaches of Stockton in July. In exchange Delta took over Transit's Cleveland Coaches subsidiary. Delta had been running Bristol REs, which were promptly sold. Stagecoach re-introduced double-deckers to the Hartlepool Transport fleet in August, with the transfer of four 1980 Fleetlines from Cleveland Transit. Hartlepool's last double-deckers were exposed-radiator Leyland PD2s delivered in 1965. Other Fleetlines on the move included seven from Cleveland and four from Busways which - rather surprisingly - headed south to join the United Counties fleet.

The attractive yellow and white Busways livery, which was initially retained by Stagecoach, finally succumbed to corporate white in June. The maroon liveried Economic operation, linking South Shields and Sunderland, is also disappearing but - for the time being at least - Favourite and Blue Bus retain their existing colours.

Back to the offices of the MMC, and Stagecoach's 20 per cent interest in Mainline of Sheffield. This produced another instruction to divest. FirstBus is to take it over, subject to approval from the Department of Trade & Industry.

In May Stagecoach announced its first interest in a mainland European operator, acquiring a shareholding in Rodoviaria de Lisboa, which operates 150 vehicles in Lisbon, Cascais, Estoril and Sintra.

The next UK acquisition, in August, ended many months of speculation about the fate of Chesterfield Transport. Mainline had expressed an interest in taking over the former municipal operation in December 1994, but this did not happen. Predictably the Stagecoach purchase of the company sounded alarm bells at the MMC and yet another investigation was launched. Whites of Calver, a Chesterfield Transport subsidiary since August 1993, was closed down. Chesterfield Transport ran 134 buses, including the Whites fleet and its Retford & District and Chesterfield Omnibus operations. It was put under East Midland management by Stagecoach.

Not all Stagecoach takeovers involve big companies. In September the 13-strong Scotravel business in Elgin was acquired by Bluebird Buses, while the 12-vehicle fleet of Warwick-based David R Grasby was taken over by Midland Red South. The Grasby name was retained. In September Midland Red South also assumed control of the 25-vehicle Vanguard business in Nuneaton, which had been bought by Stagecoach in 1993 with the Western Travel group.

Contraction by Stagecoach is rare, but happened in Manchester. The Stagecoach Manchester operation had been launched in 1994 to compete with GM Buses South following a failed attempt by Stagecoach to buy GMBS. It was cut back from 23 to 13 buses in February, and changed from B6 to B10M operation. In October it was sold, with the 13 B10Ms, to the EYMS Group and merged with the EYMS Finglands operation. The cut back in Stagecoach Manchester was part of a general outbreak of peace which saw GMBS withdraw a service to Burnley - and update its fleet with 20 nearly-new Volvo B6s on lease from Stagecoach. It was also widely seen as a prelude to a bid for GMBS by Stagecoach, although none had been made by the end of the year.

The last acquisition of 1995 was the biggest - Cambus Holdings, with 370 vehicles. Cambus Holdings was a former NBC subsidiary bought by its management in 1986. It operated as Cambus in Cambridge and Viscount in Peterborough. It also served Milton Keynes and its environs through its acquisition of Milton Keynes City Bus in 1992. This operation had in fact been the subject of some changes earlier in the year, with the merger of MKCB and its sister Buckinghamshire Road Car company, later re-named MK Metro. There was little visible sign of the change, with both Road Car and City Bus fleetnames remaining in use. MKCB was until the start of 1986 part of United Counties, another ex-NBC business which is also owned by Stagecoach.

In December the government's rail privatisation plans were in the headlines and the first passenger franchise to be awarded - South West Trains - was won by Stagecoach. SWT runs from Waterloo to Bournemouth and Exeter, and to points in between. This was the group's second incursion into railways. It had in 1992 launched the short-lived Stagecoach Rail operation, with corporate-liveried railway carriages offering cheap travel on certain Anglo-Scottish trains. On the award of the SWT franchise - for seven years from the spring of 1996 - Stagecoach reaffirmed its interest in bidding for other rail franchises. The company is a partner with the management of Network South East in Capital Coast Railways, set up to bid for Network South Central and the Gatwick Express.

New vehicles for Stagecoach in 1995 were mainly tried and tested types - large numbers of Alexander-bodied Volvo Olympians, B10Ms and Mercedes 709Ds. Subsidiaries in the north east also got Northern Counties-bodied B10Ms and Olympians, those for the Hull fleet being in Hull's smart (but threatened?) blue, yellow and white, while those for Cleveland Transit were in green, yellow and white. Cleveland, incidentally, opted to follow Busways' lead and at the end of the year announced a switch to corporate white-and-stripes. Busways received its first standard Stagecoach lowheight Alexander-bodied Olympians, with the delivery in the autumn of the first of 40.

In London, Selkent received 52 Olympians with dual-door Northern Counties bodies, the biggest single influx of new double-deckers to London for almost 10 years. East London received Dennis Darts with Alexander Dash bodies - the first Dash bodies for a former London Buses subsidiary. These were to Alexander's original Dash body style with a V-shape to the lower edge of the windscreen; a revised body with a straight windscreen line was being supplied to most Dash customers in 1995. Non-standard buses included a solitary low-floor Volvo B10L with Alexander Ultra body, which entered service with Fife Scottish in December. Further low-floor buses - Dennis Lance SLFs bodied by Berkhof - are on order for Ribble.

New coaches in 1995 were Volvo B10Ms with Plaxton Interurban bodies and the last few of an order for 50 Plaxton-bodied Dennis Javelins.

In October orders for 880 new buses for Stagecoach's UK operations were announced. These comprised 240 Olympians, 140 Volvo B10Ms, 100 Dennis Darts and 400 Mercedes-Benz 709Ds. Alexander is to supply 660 bodies, with the balance coming from Plaxton and the associated Northern Counties operation. Most exciting among the new orders were 10 B10M articulated coaches, to be fitted with Plaxton Premiere bodies.

In Africa, 50 ERF Trailblazers were delivered to Stagecoach Kenya. More are on order for 1996 for both Kenya and Malawi.

STAGECOACH HOLDINGS

Aberdare Bus Co
Bluebird Buses
    Inverness Traction
Busways Travel Services
    Armstrong Galley
    Blue Bus Services
    Economic
    Favourite Services
    Newcastle Busways
    South Shields Busways
    Sunderland Busways
    Tyne & Wear Omnibus Co
Cambus
    Millers
Cheltenham & Gloucester Omnibus Co
    City of Gloucester
    Gloucester Citybus
    Metro
    Stroud Valleys
Cheltenham District Traction
Circle Line
Cleveland Transit
    Hartlepool Transport
    KHCT
    Stagecoach Darlington
East Kent Road Car Co
East London
East Midland Motor Services
    Chesterfield Transport
Eastbourne Bus Company (New Zealand)
Fife Scottish Omnibuses
G&G Travel
Grimsby-Cleethorpes Transport
Kenya Bus Services (75 per cent)
Kenya Bus Services (Mombasa) (51 per cent)
Mainline (20 per cent)

Midland Red South
    David R Grasby
    Stratford Blue
    Vanguard Coaches
MK Metro
    Buckinghamshire Road Car
    Milton Keynes City Bus
National Transport Tokens
Premier Travel
Red & White Services
Ribble Motor Services
    Zippy
Rodoviaria de Lisboa (part)
SB Holdings (20 per cent)
Sistema Metrobus de Bogota (25 per cent)
South Coast Buses
South East London & Kent Bus Co
    Selkent
Speedybus Enterprises
Stagecoach Malawi
Stagecoach (North West)
    Cumberland Motor Services
    Coachlines
    Lakeland Experience
Stagecoach (South)
    Hampshire Bus
    Stagecoach Hants & Surrey
    Stagecoach West
Sussex Coastline
Swindon & District
United Counties Omnibus Co
    Coachlink
    Street Shuttle
The Valleys Bus Co
Viscount Bus & Coach Co
    Peterborough Bus Co
Wellington City Transport
Western Scottish Buses
    Stagecoach A1

The takeover of A1 of Ardrossan by Stagecoach led to a massive fleet replacement to get rid of time-expired buses in the A1 fleet. The first stage of this was accomplished by drafting in Leyland Titans from London, most of which ran for some time in London red. *Michael Fowler*

Upbeat show for low-floor buses

COACH & BUS 95 was the most upbeat yet in the series of events run every two years by the Confederation of Passenger Transport, the bus and coach industry's trade association. Low-floor buses were the highlight of the event, held at the National Exhibition Centre in October. There had been three low-floor buses at Coach & Bus 93 - a Wright-bodied Dennis Lance SLF, an East Lancs-bodied Scania MaxCi and a Neoplan N4014 integral.

Two years on there were 14, many of which were making their debut at the show. Dennis and Scania are in the lead, now with what might be termed second-generation models, with market leaders Volvo trailing behind.

But let's look first at that most traditional of British urban buses, the double-decker. Sales may be much lower than in the past - only 300-odd entered service in 1995 - but those on show were an interesting cross-section of what's available. Volvo's Olympian handsomely outsells all other models in this market and there were five at Coach & Bus 95 - including two for the same operator, East Yorkshire.

These were on Northern Counties' stand, where there was a 72-seat Palatine II, and with Alexander in the demonstration park, showing a long-wheelbase Royale. Both were in the new crimson and cream livery adopted by East Yorkshire in 1995 to replace its previous red and grey scheme. A standard Northern Counties Palatine I, but with two-door layout, was on show in the livery of Stagecoach subsidiary Selkent. It was a 68-seater with room for 20 standees.

Two other Alexander-bodied Olympians demonstrated the versatility of the double-deck bus. On Alexander's stand there was a giant three-axle air-conditioned vehicle for Hong Kong Citybus. Its carrying capacity was a massive 135 - 56 upstairs, 42 downstairs and 37 standees. And Volvo

exhibited one of a fleet of high-specification long-wheelbase Olympians for London United. These have Alexander Royale bodies and are for use on the Airbus service linking Heathrow Airport with Central London. There are 43 seats on the top deck and just nine, rather claustrophobic, seats at the rear of the lower saloon. The bulk of the

An artist's impression of the new Northern Counties low-floor Paladin LF body. The finished product actuall looked considerably better...

The new East Lancs Cityzen is based on Scania's N113 chassis. The bus was launched with an order from Northumbria Motor Services.
David Barrow

The Dennis Dart SLF was one of the talking points of the show. Those on display had revised Plaxton Pointer bodies which are lower and wider - 2.4m compared with 2.3m - than the original Pointers. *Stewart J Brown*

lower deck area is given over to luggage racks. The new Airbuses are air-conditioned and can carry wheelchair passengers. Their high specification means a high unladen weight - 12,740kg - which may well make them Britain's heaviest-ever double-deck buses.

Dennis used Coach & Bus 95 to unveil its new Lance double-decker. This is based on the single-deck chassis of the same name, with the main differences being an uprated suspension system and a 5050mm wheelbase for an overall bodied length of 10.5m. The show bus, the first to be built, had a Northern Counties Palatine II body with 79 seats and was the first of a pair for Nottingham City Transport. All of the seats are forward facing. The Lance weighed 10,840kg.

The lightest double-decker, according to the lettering on the side, was the new Scania-East Lancs Cityzen, at 10,030kg. The Cityzen is the second joint project between the two companies -the

first was the short-lived low-floor MaxCi, which has been overtaken by the simpler (and spectacularly more attractive) Axcess-ultralow. The 78-seat Cityzen is based on a standard Scania N113 chassis with a 220bhp 11-litre transverse rear engine and Voith automatic gearbox, but the body is a complete break with East Lancs' tradition. It was styled by John Worker Design, best known in the bus and coach business for the Duple 425 Integral.

Split single-curvature windscreens are used on the front lower deck to keep replacement costs down, and these are flanked by deep flat glass side screens to give good all-round visibility from the driving seat. On the upper deck front a single-piece double-curvature screen is used, with a separate full-width glazed section below it to house the destination display. The show model, the first of 13 for Northumbria Motor Services, had tinted glazing, using square-cornered gasket-mounting. Bonded side windows are to be offered as an option.

A potentially significant new double-deck chassis was shown by DAF, in what had to be the lowest-key launch of the decade. It was a low-floor double-decker, and used the front frame of a new low-floor single-deck model which was being exhibited by Northern Counties.

Will low-floor double-deckers be the big talking point at Coach & Bus 97?

The single-deck market is clearly in the throes of change. There were 23 buses in the exhibition hall of which 14 were of low-floor layout and nine were based on conventional chassis. The latter included two Volvo B10Bs, a Wright-bodied 49-seater for Merseybus (the operator's 100th Wright body) and a Plaxton-bodied 51-seater for City of Oxford. On Optare's stand there was an example of the new Prisma on the Mercedes-Benz O405 chassis for Tees & District, part of North East Bus. A similar vehicle for Grampian Transport was exhibited by Mercedes. The simpler steel-suspended Mercedes OH1416 was also on display and had an attractive Wright Urbanranger body. It was a 47-seater for Midland Choice. Few OH1416s have been sold since the model's launch in mid-1994 when Mercedes was optimistically looking for sales of 50 a year.

While Dennis used the show to launch its new low-floor Dart, two bodybuilders showed existing Darts. On the Alexander stand there was a 36-seat 9.8m Dash for East London, one of a batch of 27 and the first Dashes to receive London red livery. And UVG (previously WS Coachbuilders and before that Wadham Stringer) showed its new Urban Star body, a 36-seater in the colours of Provincial, which just prior to the show had become part of the FirstBus group. Interestingly both the Alexander and UVG Darts weighed the same, 6260kg.

The new UVG body - another John Worker Design style - certainly shakes off the somewhat utilitarian look of previous bodies produced at the company's Waterlooville factory. The steel-framed Portsdown was not exactly a runaway sales success. The Urban Star is 2.4m wide and uses Cromweld stainless steel framing. An interesting design feature is the dip in the nearside windscreen, designed to improve visibility. The Urban Star is also being offered on the Volvo B6 and MAN 11.190 chassis.

The low-floor Dennis Dart SLF was undoubtedly one of the talking points of the show, not least because it offers full accessibility at a much lower price than most other low-floor buses. It overshadowed Volvo's B6LE, announced earlier in the year but living in the shadow of the reputation of the original B6, which has not always been the most reliable of buses. A B6LE in the livery of GM Buses North was shown on the Wright stand. A 37-seater, it weighed 8360kg. Plaxton also showed a B6LE demonstrator with the new, wider, Pointer body.

There was one low-floor Lance SLF, a 70-passenger two-door bus in BAA colours for operation at Heathrow Airport. Bodied by Berkhof, it was one of 30 delivered during the year and operated on BAA's behalf by Speedlink Airport Services. They brought new standards of accessibility to the airport's inter-terminal services. The Lance SLF looks as though it may become a victim of the success of the 10.5m-long Super Dart SLF.

Four Scania L113 single-deckers were on show. Two were stylish Axcess-ultralows, bodied by Wright - one for Rider York's park-and-ride services, the other for Bullock of Cheadle. There was also a boxy-looking East Lancs-bodied bus for The Shires. An L113 for Trans Island Bus Services in Singapore was on the Alexander stand. It was a 45-seat two-door bus with air-conditioning and an interior which made extensive use of light green trim, reminiscent of Alexander bodies for Glasgow Corporation Transport in the 1960s. The body was based on the Strider, but featured square-cornered glazing and a revised front panel which combined to transform its appearance. In the demonstration park there was a reminder of Scania's first attempt at an accessible bus in the shape of an East Lancs-bodied MaxCi. Even Scania's smart new two-tone blue demonstration livery couldn't turn what looks like a bit of a pig's ear into something approaching a silk purse.

Volvo's B10L, launched in 1994, picked up two significant orders in 1995. The first, from Ulsterbus, called for 60 with Alexander Ultra bodywork. One of these, in Citybus colours, was on show, as was a similar vehicle for Stagecoach's Fife Scottish operation. Volvo used the show to announce another low-floor chassis, the B10BLE which will offer ease of access at a lower price than the B10L and follows the lead taken by Dennis and Scania in adapting conventional single-deck chassis to produce easy-access buses. The B10BLE will use the independent front suspension of the B10L but the rear end of the B10B. Will it kill sales of the B10L? The other B10L order, incidentally, came from West Midlands Travel, which is to take 100 with bodywork by Wright - and which suggests that it may be a bit premature to speculate on the fate of the B10L.

Sales of DAF single-deckers have been steady if unspectacular, with Ikarus-bodied SB220s appearing in small numbers, and generally in smallish fleets. The appearance of a low-floor SB220 was one of the surprises of the show, as was the attractive Northern Counties body fitted to it. Novel body features included glass fibre side panels and an electrically-operated roller destination blind which combines the legibility of old destination screen technology with the convenience of electric power to change it. This bus was a two-door demonstrator and the body can be expected to appear on other chassis during 1996. The low-frame SB220 has a horizontal version of DAF's RS200 8.65-litre engine, rather than the bigger 11.6 used in the standard SB220. This engine was first seen in Britain (in vertical form) in the Optare Spectra.

The big news on the coach front was the launch of a new Iveco range, the EuroRider with bodywork by Beulas, a Spanish builder. The front-engined Iveco EuroMidi was also on show with Indcar bodywork. This is Iveco's first serious attack on the British coach market and only time will tell if they have more success with coaches than they have had in the bus business.

New on the Plaxton stand was an Excalibur based on a three-axle Volvo B12 chassis - Plaxton's first three-axle coach since the Bedford VAL. It was an impressive vehicle and was destined for Dodsworth of Boroughbridge. Volvo's new B10M SE chassis, which has a revised frame layout to offer more luggage capacity, was on show with a Plaxton Premiere body in National Express livery. It was a Durham Travel Services coach.

MarcoPolo bodywork made its first appearance at the NEC on a Dennis Javelin chassis for Coach Stop of Leigh-on-Sea. MarcoPolo is a major Brazilian builder with a factory in Portugal and this is the first time the company's products have been offered in the UK. The MarcoPolo body is only available on the Javelin chassis through DSB Sales, the Leicestershire-based Dennis dealer.

Javelin coach sales rose by 54 per cent in 1995 and other examples on show had bodywork by Plaxton, Neoplan, Berkhof and Caetano. The last-named showed a basic specification Porto body, aimed at the lower end of the coach market seeking a no-frills vehicle for private hires. It had a split windscreen and flat glass side windows. At the other extreme there was the first Javelin to carry a Plaxton Excalibur body - destined for a Maltese operator and the first new British coach to be shipped to Malta for many a long year. In the demonstration park there was a Javelin with UVG UniStar coach bodywork, developed from the Wadham Stringer Vanguard III. UVG have worked hard to make what started life as a bus look like a coach. The measure of their success will be the sales it achieves.

The Volvo B10M is Britain's best-selling coach and apart from Plaxton-bodied examples, there were B10Ms with bodywork by Caetano, Jonckheere and Van Hool. The Jonckheere coach was the first of an attractive new design, the Mistral, and was for Clarkes of London. However the Mistral will not be generally available in Britain until 1997 - which might just put a damper on Jonckheere's UK sales in 1996.

Scania has invested considerable effort in promoting the impressive Irizar Century body, and with a high degree of success. Two were on show - a three-axle K113TRB for Gary Dixon of Wolverhampton, and a two-axle K113CRB for C&G of Chatteris. The high-specification Gary Dixon coach was the heaviest single-deck at the show, weighing 14,870kg - a figure exceeded only by a Neoplan Skyliner double-decker for Impact of Carlisle at 16,580kg.

There were two DAF SB3000s on show, one bodied by Berkhof and the other with a new Ikarus body which should be available in Britain in 1996. Van Hool showed two EOS (ex-LAG) integrals, a short, 41-seat 80 demonstrator, and a standard 12m 49-seat 90 for Gain Travel. There were also two Bovas, a high-floor coach for Moor-Dale, and a low-floor model for Andy James, the Wiltshire operator. Setra had two of its expensive - but high-quality - S250s on show, including one in an eye-catching livery for Boons of Boreham. There was one MAN, on the Berkhof stand, a demonstration 11.190 35-seat midi.

Front-engined minibuses were primarily based on the market-leading Mercedes T2 range, and included Alexander Sprints for Cumberland and Midland Red North, two UVG Wessex minis (in the process of being rechristened the Citi Star) for Rhondda and a Plaxton Beaver for Bristol City Line. This was a prototype on a new air-suspended chassis, designed to offer lower steps and due to be launched in 1996. A UVG-bodied Iveco 59.12 was on show for Bluebird of Manchester. Optare's MetroRider was represented by a 31-seater for Trent, a regular buyer for a wide range of Optare products. This was the 2,000th MetroRider, a figure which includes those built by MCW as well as the more recent output from the Optare factory.

A bargain basement mini from India was shown by TATA. The 27-seat DB709 uses a 90bhp 3.8-litre four-cylinder TATA engine. TATA may be little known in Europe, but they build around 140,000 trucks and buses a year. It is unlikely that many will find their way to Britain, unless as welfare vehicles.

There were two new small coaches. Autobus Classique was showing its new range, the Nouvelle, on Mercedes chassis. This features a new front end to disguise the coach's humble origins on a modified light truck chassis. Similarly the Italian built Cacciamali offered a stylish alternative on Mercedes or Iveco chassis.

Cummins gave UK operators their first view of the 11-litre M11 engine. It's been used in trucks in the USA for a couple of years and is seen as a replacement for the 10-litre L10. As yet no bus or coach chassis makers have announced its availability for vehicles offered in the UK market. Indeed Volvo, the main user of the L10 (in the Olympian) announced that it is to cease offering the option of Cummins power.

All in all, Coach & Bus 95 was a show with lots going on. It showed that the British bus and coach market is far from being in the doldrums - which it certainly was at the start of the 1990s - with exciting new models from a number of makers.

What was missing? There were no DAF double-deckers (although there was the low-floor chassis), and the Dennis Dominator was absent too. Few of the latter are being built - production is nearing an end - although the three-axle export variants continue to enjoy healthy sales. There were no MAN buses, although there was a chassis and the announcement of the low-floor NL222FR for 1996. There were no Blue Birds either. And does anyone remember the Oasa 903? One was in the demonstration park at Coach & Bus 93. Built in the Czech Republic, it didn't re-appear at Coach & Bus 95. It wasn't missed.

A low-cost Dennis Javelin coach was exhibited by Caetano. The Porto body features flat glass side windows and a two-piece windscreen among other cost-saving items. *Stewart J Brown*

New buses in London

Stagecoach added new buses to both its London fleets. East London got Dennis Darts while Selkent received 52 Volvo Olympians. The Darts were bodied by Alexander; the Olympians by Northern Counties. *Peter Rowlands*

THE PRIVATISATION OF NBC and of SBG was followed by a dearth of new buses. The newly-privatised companies were, generally, too short of cash in their early days of independence to invest in new vehicles. The situation in London has been rather different, with a number of the privatised companies being sold to established groups with the financial muscle to inject new buses into their London fleets.

The privatisation of London Buses was in fact only completed in January 1995, when the sale of South London to the Cowie Group - owners of Grey-Green and Leaside Buses - was concluded. This made Cowie London's biggest bus operator, with a combined fleet of over 1,000 vehicles between its three subsidiaries. Stagecoach had ended up with two London Buses companies on opposite sides of the Thames - East London and Selkent, with not far short of 1,000 buses between them. Two other

provincially-based groups got one company each with London Northern going to MTL Trust Holdings and London Central to the Gateshead-based Go-Ahead Group. Birmingham-based West Midlands Travel bought Stanwell Buses from its management just a few weeks after the company's privatisation in the early part of 1994. This left four former London Buses subsidiaries as substantial independents in the control of management/employee buy-outs - CentreWest, London General, London United and Metroline.

MTL strengthened its London operations during 1995 with two acquisitions. In April it bought London Suburban (and the associated Liverbus operation in Liverpool). London Suburban had been set up by Liverbus to run LT tendered services, starting operations in September 1993. Its 51-strong fleet was made up mainly of ex-London Titans and new Volvo Olympians with Northern Counties Palatine II bodies. In October MTL bought another north London operator, R&I, which had been running tendered routes since 1989. R&I had started as an operator of small coaches and at the time of the MTL takeover its fleet comprised 39 buses -mainly Dennis Darts - and 25 coaches. The coach operation is being rebranded Sightseers London. MTL coaches in Liverpool run under the Sightseers name.

West Midlands Travel obviously had second thoughts about the wisdom of running buses

The Airbus service between Heathrow Airport and Central London was transformed by the arrival of the first of a new generation of air-conditioned double-deckers to replace elderly MCW Metrobuses. The new Airbuses have Volvo Olympian chassis and Alexander Royale bodies.

in London, and in September sold the 131-vehicle Stanwell Buses to London United - the company's third change of ownership in just 20 months. Metroline expanded its coaching activities in August with the purchase of Brents of Watford, which continues as an autonomous operation. One other expansion was by CentreWest, which won tenders in the Bexley area - giving it routes and an operating base remote from its main centre of operation in west London.

The changes in 1995 have reduced the number of large independents running buses in and around London to just four (not counting the privatised London Buses subsidiaries) - Armchair, Capital Citybus, London Buslines and Metrobus. All of the others which might appear to be independent are related to groups such as Blazefield Holdings, British Bus and Cowie. Capital Citybus was, until a buy-out in December, owned by the much larger Hong Kong Citybus company.

Modified liveries have marked the changes of ownership of the former London Buses companies. Stagecoach has adopted all-over red for most types, although Routemasters have a cream relief band and in a nice gesture towards their antiquity they carry gold rather than white fleetnames. MTL London Northern has opted for all-over red on all types of vehicles, and this is also being applied to the London Suburban and R&I fleets - the former was absorbed into the MTL London Northern operation in October. London General has retained the grey skirt used by London Buses, but added a yellow stripe above it. London United has also retained the grey skirt, but brightened its fleet by the addition of white relief for the roof and top-deck window surrounds on double-deckers. Metroline has added blue relief to its buses, while Leaside has added yellow.

Thus red, as might be expected, continues to dominate London's streets - and more red may be on the way with LT insisting that buses used on new tenders in the central area must feature red in

their liveries. This does not apply to existing tenders - at least not until they come up for renewal. Stagecoach's East London operation raised a few eyebrows when Titans in corporate white livery appeared in service. But no, it wasn't another fleet changing to corporate colours. It was rather a sensible repaint in Stagecoach livery for vehicles scheduled for early transfer to companies elsewhere in the group.

New buses were delivered to a number of London fleets during 1995. The biggest intake was by Selkent, which received a fleet of 52 new Volvo Olympians with

two-door Northern Counties bodies. Northern Counties-bodied Olympians were also bought by CentreWest and by London Central, the latter in addition taking a batch with Alexander Royale bodies. London Central's Royales were the first in the capital, but they were joined in the autumn by a dozen for London United, which ordered long-wheelbase chassis to be fitted with air-conditioned bodies for use on the Airbus service between Heathrow Airport and central London. These eye-catching buses have 52 seats - 43 on the top deck and just nine below, located at the rear of the

London's first Volvo B6 was this Wright-bodied B6LE demonstrator in London General livery. It was an exhibit at the UITP public transport show in Paris in May and is seen here before entering service.

The closure of London Underground's East London Line saw replacement bus services being provided by East London and Capital Citybus. The buses used on the replacement services carry a yellow and white livery as shown on this Capital Citybus Leyland Olympian. It has an Alexander body and was new to Highland Scottish. *Stewart J Brown*

Route		Previous operator	New operator
61	Bromley North - Chiselhurst	Metrobus	CentreWest
81	Hounslow - Slough	London Buslines	Westlink
138	Catford Bridge - Coney Hall	Kentish Bus	Metrobus
161	Woolwich - Chiselhurst	Kentish Bus	Metrobus
R1	Bromley Common - St Pauls Cray	Selkent	CentreWest
R2	Petts Wood - Biggin Hill Valley	Selkent	Crystals
R3	Petts Wood - Green Street Green	Selkent	CentreWest
R4	Locks Bottom - Pauls Cray Hill	Selkent	CentreWest
R7	Petts Wood - St Mary Cray	Kentish Bus	Crystals
R8	Cockmannings - Chelsfield	Selkent	Londonlinks
R11	QM Hosp - Green Street Green	Selkent	CentreWest
S3	Worcester Park - Belmont	-	Tellings Golden Miller

saloon behind cavernous luggage racks. Wheelchair lifts are concealed beneath the entrance step, continuing a policy of making the Airbus service accessible to disabled travellers. The new London United Olympians replaced ageing Metrobuses.

The Northern Counties bodies for Selkent and London Central were Palatine Is, based on the company's established double-deck design, albeit with a revised (one hesitates to say improved) upper deck front featuring peaked windows. The more stylish Palatine II was specified by Leaside Buses, which took 13 on DAF DB250 chassis. Cowie, the owners of Leaside, also own Hughes DAF, the distributor for the DB250/Northern Counties combination.

Single-deck deliveries to London continue to be dominated by Dennis Darts. Darts with Plaxton bodies were delivered to CentreWest, Leaside and London

General. The first Alexander-bodied Darts to carry London red were 27 for Stagecoach's East London fleet. The only other single-deckers for a former London Buses operation were eight MAN 11.190s with Optare Vecta bodies which joined the Stanwell Buses fleet. Similar buses were bought by R&I before its takeover by MTL. Twelve MANs, but with Marshall bodies, have been ordered by MTL for delivery in 1996 for use on the 95 service.

There were no new low-floor bus orders in 1995 to follow on from the 68 which were among the last orders placed by London Buses and which took to the capital's streets in 1994. A Wright-bodied Volvo B6LE entered trial service with London General after being exhibited at the UITP exhibition in Paris in the spring. A low-floor Dart SLF with two-door Plaxton Pointer body was exhibited by Dennis at Coach & Bus 95 in the colours of CentreWest, to enter

trial service in the early part of 1996.

On route tendering the first service ever to have been won by an independent was the 81 from Hounslow to Slough, back in July 1985 when it was taken over by London Buslines with a fleet of new Leyland Lynxes. After 10 years operation by London Buslines it changed operators in July 1995, passing to Westlink which used Optare Deltas from its existing fleet.

Tellings Golden Miller won a minibus service in March, the new S3 linking Worcester Park and Belmont. Three new Mercedes with Plaxton Beaver bodies were bought for this operation. Crystals of Orpington took delivery of six Mercedes with Crystals bodies for its newly-won tendered services. The Stationlink service was re-tendered in 1995 and retained by Frank E Thorpe, but with a switch from Mercedes minibuses to new low-floor single-deckers planned from February 1996.

London Underground's East London line was closed in the spring for extensive refurbishment and two contracts were awarded for replacement bus services, using vehicles in a distinctive yellow and white livery. Capital Citybus won one of the contracts with a fleet of double-deckers - mainly Alexander-bodied Dominators and Olympians which had come from Scottish operators. The other contract went to East London using Optare StarRiders.

Selkent lost a number of Orpington tendered routes in the autumn,. most going to CentreWest, which set up a new operating base in the area. It bought a fleet of 36 new buses for the services - 12 Northern Counties-bodied Olympians, 17 Plaxton-bodied Darts and seven Marshall-bodied Mercedes.

Problems in maintaining service reliability led to four Kentish Bus routes being taken over by Metrobus. Two changed operator in December, with a further two to follow in January 1996. Metrobus acquired some vehicles from Kentish Bus to run the services.

Route		Existing operator	New operator
67	Wood Green - Aldgate	Leaside Buses	Capital Citybus
95	Southall - Shepherd's Bush	CentreWest	MTL London Northern
105	Heathrow Central - Greenford	CentreWest	London & Country
106	Finsbury Park - Whitechapel	Leaside Buses	Docklands Transit
181	Lewisham - Downham	Kentish Bus	Metrobus
191	Brimsdown - Edmonton Green	Leaside Buses	Thamesway
258	Watford Junction - South Harrow	Luton & District	London Buslines
263	Archway - Barnet General Hospital	MTL London Northern	Leaside Buses
284	Lewisham - Grove Park	Kentish Bus	Metrobus
399	Barnet General Hospital circular	Welwyn-Hatfield	Thamesway
473	North Woolwich - Stratford	Grey-Green	East London
678	East Beckton - Stratford	East London	Capital Citybus
C10	Victoria - Elephant & Castle	London General	London Buslines

Iveco launch EuroCoaches

IVECO LAUNCHED ITS first attack on the UK coach market in October with the new EuroRider chassis, carrying high-specification bodywork by Spanish builders Beulas. And, despite the failure of its TurboCity bus to find any orders, it still has the bus business in its sights, promising a EuroRider fitted with a new design of Marshall interurban bus bodywork. This is to appear in 1996.

The EuroRider is produced in Spain at what was the Pegaso factory - Pegaso has been part of the Iveco group since 1991. The first model being offered to UK operators is a two-axle 12m variant. It will be followed in 1996 with a three-axle version suitable for coach bodywork up to 3.7m high. The pressed steel chassis has a conventional straight frame with a height of 726mm above the ground. This compares with, for example, 790mm for a Volvo B10M in the area aft of the engine. For bus use this can be lowered by modifying the suspension and fitting low-profile tyres to provide a maximum gangway height of 650mm.

The engine is a turbocharged vertical Iveco 8460.41S 9.5-litre unit manufactured in France. It is mounted at the rear and meets Euro 2 exhaust emission standards. Two power ratings are offered for coach operation, 290bhp in the EuroRider 391.12.29 and 345bhp in the 391.12.35. The middle figures indicate the overall length; the final figures the power output. A 260bhp option will be available for the interurban bus. A ZF manual gearbox is used for coaches - the S6-85 on the 290bhp model and the eight-speed 8S-180 on the 345bhp chassis. A ZF 5HP600 automatic is standard for the bus and an option on the lower powered coach. Chassis with automatic gearboxes have an A suffix added to the model code.

Air suspension is fitted with a ferry-lift facility and, on interurban models, a kneeling device. ZF power steering is standard. The EuroRider has a Telma retarder and anti-lock braking

Beulas has been building bodies since 1934 and the first EuroRiders for British operators have attractively-styled 3.425m-high bodies with a distinctive down-sweep on the front side windows. The rear-view mirrors are of the fashionable floppy rabbit's ears type. Air-conditioning is standard and there is a choice of interior seating layouts. A plug door is fitted and the overall effect is of a modern coach in the European idiom. The first two, shown at Coach & Bus 95, were for Channel Coachways of London and Coliseum Coaches of Southampton. Beulas build around 200 coaches annually.

The EuroRider chassis can be made available for coaches up to 15m long - a type beginning to be seen on the European mainland - and as an articulated 18m interurban vehicle.

The EuroRider could just be the break into big vehicles which Iveco has been looking for, and its arrival in the UK followed the launch earlier in the year of a truck-derived midicoach which started life as the CountryBus but was quickly renamed the EuroMidi. It is a development of the EuroCargo and like all Iveco models has a complex model code - CC95.9E18F. The 18 is the power output - 177bhp - rounded up to the nearest ten. This power comes from a 5.9-litre turbocharged Iveco 8060.45B engine which sits alongside the driver. A six-speed synchromesh gearbox is standard, with an Allison AT545 automatic as an option.

The EuroMidi has a 4635mm wheelbase and is designed for bodywork up to 9.7m long and 2.5m wide. A set-back front axle allows the provision of an entrance in the front overhang. It has steel suspension, small (17.5in) wheels and an air-hydraulic braking system. The first EuroMidis in Britain have been bodied by Indcar, another Spanish builder and one was shown at the Brighton Coach Rally in April and at Coach & Bus 95 in October.

The Indcar body is steel-framed, air-conditioned - an unusual luxury on a coach in this class - and the first for the UK had 35 reclining seats. Iveco say that the chassis can also be bodied by Mellor and UVG.

The next new product which Iveco plans for the UK is its low-floor CityClass urban bus chassis. It is due to appear in 1997.

Iveco's most serious attempt yet in the UK market for full-sized vehicles came with the launch of the Beulas-bodied EuroRider. Coliseum Coaches of Southampton was among the first to order one.

FirstBus - a new name in buses

GRT ordered high-specification buses for a number of its fleets including Leicester Citybus. This is a Mercedes-Benz O405 with Optare Prisma bodywork and MAC-Hispacold air conditioning housed in a neat pod on the roof. It is one of 10 in the Leicester fleet.

THE NEW NAME in buses in 1995 was FirstBus - an amalgamation of Badgerline, with its headquarters in Avon, and GRT Bus Group, based at the other end of the country in Aberdeen. The deal was announced in May, and FirstBus started off with a fleet of 5,600 vehicles of which some 4,000 came from Badgerline, by far the bigger partner in the organisation. The FirstBus title is an aspiration rather than a fact.

The combination brought together two rather different operations. GRT had a corporate identity, using a cream-based livery with different relief colours for each of its main operating companies. The limit of Badgerline's corporate image was the use of a badger logo on the group's buses. After the amalgamation the badger logos were quickly removed from most buses, except those run by Badgerline Ltd. Similarly the thistle logo used by GRT - in place of a dot above the letter "i" - was abandoned. A statement on a new corporate FirstBus identity was expected to be announced in 1996.

Vehicle policies were somewhat different too. Badgerline had standardised on Plaxton bodywork for most of its vehicles, on Dennis chassis for single-deckers and on Mercedes for minis. It did in 1995 buy from other builders too, most notably Alexander, on a batch of 50 Dennis Darts for Yorkshire Rider - a company which had in recent pre-Badgerline years bought a fair number of bodies from the Scottish coachbuilder. The only double-deckers on order for Badgerline were 33 Alexander-bodied Volvo Olympians which were part of the group's £60 million order announced in the summer of 1994. However these did not materialise.

GRT Bus Group was ordering smaller numbers of buses, but to a high specification which for some companies included double-glazing and air-conditioning. These were on Mercedes O405 and Scania chassis, with bodywork by Wright and Optare, both of which use the Alusuisse system of aluminium extrusions for their body structures. Thus each group was supporting different chassis and body manufacturers in the run up to the creation of FirstBus. It will be interesting to see which manufacturers benefit when the first FirstBus vehicle order is announced.

Prior to the formation of FirstBus, GRT made the news with the launch in January of Britain's first commercially-served guided busway, at Kesgrave, near Ipswich. It is a short stretch of bus-only road, built to accommodate Dennis Darts fitted with lateral guidewheels. The last guided busway in Britain was in the West Midlands in the days before deregulation.

In May Badgerline's Western National subsidiary took over two small Cornish businesses - Brookside Travel of Relubbus and Lidgeys Coaches of Tregony. Other small takeovers by FirstBus in 1995 saw Midland Bluebird buy Kings of Dunblane in July, and Brewers acquiring the coach operations of Cardiff City Transport in November. Thamesway took over District Bus which had briefly been in the ownership of British Bus. One small business was disposed of. Frontline of Tamworth, a Badgerline company, was sold to British Bus in the summer.

In the summer FirstBus stepped forward as the candidate to take over Stagecoach's 20 per cent stake in Mainline, as Stagecoach complied with an MMC ruling that it dispose of its Mainline shareholding. This acquisition was agreed in December, subject to approval by the Department of Trade and Industry.

September saw Yorkshire Rider, with over 1,000 vehicles the biggest FirstBus subsidiary, being split into four autonomous units - Leeds City Link, Bradford Traveller, Calderline (in Halifax and Todmorden) and Kingfisher in Huddersfield. They retained existing Yorkshire Rider colours, pending a decision by FirstBus on a corporate livery. Buses in Leeds had Yorkshire Rider names removed and generally ran anonymously, few receiving Leeds City Link branding. Elsewhere the new names replaced the old.

As this was happening the second guided busway of 1995 was opened in Leeds. Sited on the A61, it was the first phase of a planned series of bus priorities. Ridership on the routes using the busway rose by nine per cent in just two months.

The only significant expansion by FirstBus in 1995 was announced in October, with the purchase of Provincial of Fareham. Provincial, a unique buy-out of an NBC subsidiary by an employee co-operative, had been in the private sector since 1987 and ran 155 buses, predominantly Leyland Nationals. New buses in the fleet were generally Iveco Ford minis, but there was also a solitary ACE Cougar midibus, with locally-manufactured Wadham Stringer body.

In marked contrast to the split-up of Yorkshire Rider into smaller units was the re-unification of Badgerline and Bristol Omnibus into a single company in November. The Badgerline and City Line trading names are to be retained. A similar event was announced in December with the formation of Essex Buses to re-unite Eastern National and Thamesway. Again the separate trading names and liveries are to be retained.

New buses in 1995 were based on existing orders placed by GRT and Badgerline. The Rider Group started the year with the beginning of the inflow of a remarkable 179 buses - 48 Dennis Lances, 68 Dennis Darts and 63 Mercedes-Benz 709D

minibuses - delivery of which was spread through to the autumn. Of these new buses, 110 were allocated to Huddersfield, giving the town one of Britain's most modern bus fleets.

Lances with Plaxton Verde bodies were also added to the Midland Red West and PMT fleets. Five low-floor Lance SLFs, bodied by Wright, were delivered to Badgerline for operation in Bath. One similar bus went to Western National. Plaxton-bodied Darts were taken into a number of fleets: Badgerline, Brewers, Bristol City Line, Eastern National, Midland Red West, Thamesway and Western National. Thamesway also received four Darts with Marshall bodywork. Dennises figured in coach purchases with a number being used on National Express services from the West Country and South Wales. The group's biggest single coach order came from Thamesway, which received 19 Volvo B10Ms with Plaxton Premiere bodies.

Rider York received the bulk of an order for 20 of Scania's new Axcess-ultralow, with Wright bodywork on L113 chassis. They were used on upgraded park-and-ride services in the city.

The former GRT companies

received rather different types. Mercedes-Benz O405s with Optare Prisma bodies were delivered to Eastern Scottish, Grampian Transport and Leicester Citybus. right-bodied Scanias were added to two Scottish fleets, Lowland and Midland Bluebird. Dennis Darts - a model not widely used by GRT - were delivered to Grampian at the end of the year. They had Alexander bodies and were in place of a planned batch of Mercedes minibuses. Alexander-bodied Mercedes 709Ds were delivered to Eastern Counties and Midland Bluebird.

Northampton Transport received the first production Volvo B10Ls for a British operator, putting three into operation in the autumn. They had Alexander Ultra bodywork, built in Belfast to Swedish designs. The B10L is a low-floor chassis and these buses had been ordered by GRT.

The first purpose-built CNG-powered bus in Britain was completed during the year, but was not to be unveiled until 1996. It was a Plaxton-bodied Dart and was to operate in Bristol alongside conventional diesel-fuelled examples.

Rider York ordered 20 Scania Axcess-ultralows for use on upgraded park-and-ride services in York city. It made the company the biggest user of the type in 1995. The Axcess-ultralow has bodywork by Wright. *Michael Fowler*

FIRSTBUS	
Aberdeen Bus (not trading)	Mairs of Aberdeen
Badgerline	Midland Bluebird
Brewers	Midland Red West
Bristol Omnibus Co	Midland Red Coaches
City Line	Northampton Transport
Durbin	Oban & District*
Broch Cymru	PMT
(Badger Wales) †	Crosville
Eastern Counties	Pennine
Rosemary Coaches	Red Rider
Eastern Scottish Omnibuses	Rider Group
SMT Edinburgh	Bradford Traveller
SMT Lothians	Calderline
SMT Coaches	Gold Rider
Eastern National	Kingfisher
Grampian Transport	Leeds City Link
Kirkpatrick of Deeside	Quickstep Travel
Leicester Citybus	Rider York
Lowland Omnibuses	South Wales Transport
Ian Glass	Thamesway
Lothian Transit	Wessex Coaches
Mainline Group (20%)	Sky Blue
	Western National
* minority shareholding	Roberts
† not trading	

SHEFFIELD WAS ONE of the flash points in deregulated Britain. It attracted a lot of new operators, the town centre was over-bussed, and South Yorkshire Transport's willingness to purchase its competitors led to a four-year battle with the Monopolies and Mergers Commission which ended with victory for SYT - although only after taking the matter to the High Court.

SYT had, in 1989, taken over five of the operators running bus services in the city - Groves Coaches, Richardson, Sheaf Line, Sheffield & District (owned by Caldaire) and SUT, which was part of the short-lived ATL group. To this it added the Don Valley business, in 1991. In October 1992 Yorkshire Traction bought Andrews, which ran 50 double-deckers, and followed this in November 1994 with the 34-bus South Riding operation.

This meant that at the start of 1995 there were two significant independents in the city. The older of the two was Yorkshire Terrier, set up in 1988 with 12 Leyland Nationals and by 1995 running a 65-strong fleet which included modern Dennis Darts and Volvo B6s. The newer was Sheffield Omnibus, formed at the start of 1991 with a fleet of seven ex-

Preston Atlanteans. Sheffield Omnibus retained Preston's cream and blue livery, applying it to subsequent additions to the fleet which coincidentally included Atlanteans from the other Preston-based bus company, Ribble. Sheffield Omnibus also bought new B6s as well as new Leyland Olympians and Volvo B10M buses. Its fleet numbered 95 vehicles at the start of 1995.

Sheffield Omnibus had set up an operation in Nottingham in July 1993 - Nottingham Omnibus. It ran just over 30 buses, also in Preston-inspired livery, and closed in June 1994.

In April 1995 both Yorkshire Terrier and Sheffield Omnibus were bought by Yorkshire Traction, significantly strengthening the company's position in the city which is now effectively served by just two operators - Mainline and Yorkshire Traction's various subsidiaries. The first signs of rationalisation came in the summer with the appearance of buses carrying combined Andrews Sheffield Omnibus fleetnames, in a blue and cream livery.

Mainline - as South Yorkshire Transport became in 1993 - has been quietly rationalising its operations, absorbing Sheaf Line

In April Yorkshire Terrier and Sheffield Omnibus were both bought by Yorkshire Traction. The newest buses in both fleets were Volvo B6s with Alexander Dash bodies. The bus on the right shows the new Andrews Sheffield Omnibus livery adopted in the summer as Yorkshire Traction combined the workings of two of its Sheffield companies. *L M Whitehead.*

and Don Valley Buses into the main fleet during the year. Both had initially been retained as separate operating units under Mainline ownership. Mainline also took a 10 per cent stake in Northern Bus in January, now the only significant independent operator running regularly into Sheffield.

The operators acquired by Yorkshire Traction had all started by running second-hand buses, although the bigger fleets had moved on to investment in new vehicles. Yorkshire Traction has updated its Sheffield fleets with a mixture of new buses and vehicles transferred from other parts of the group. The companies acquired by SYT ran few new vehicles, but older buses have been disposed of and Mainline has a strong record of investment in new buses - most noticeably Volvo B10Ms with Alexander PS-type bodies.

The signs are that Sheffield's days as England's most over-bussed city are over for good.

Who makes what

A guide to chassis available to UK operators in 1995, or announced in 1995 with availability for 1996.

Make and model	Engine Position	Overall Length (m)	Wheel base (m)	Engine	Cubic capacity (l)	Power (bhp)	Gearbox	Speeds
BLUE BIRD (USA)								
Q-Bus	RV	11.5	6.32	Cummins B	5.9	190	Allison MT545	4 A
BOVA integrals (Holland)								
Futura FHD	RV	12.0	6.09	DAF WS242	11.6	329	ZF S6-85	6 M
Futura Club FLC	RV	12.0	6.09	Cummins C	8.3	275	ZF S6-85	6 M
Futura Club FLD	RV	12.0	6.09	DAF RS200L	8.65	272	ZF S6-85	6 M
DAF (Holland)								
DB250	RV	10.2	5.05	DAF RS200	8.65	272	ZF 4HP500	4 A
SB220	RH	11.8	5.50	DAF LT160L	11.6	218	ZF 4HP500	4 A
SB220GS	RH	11.9	6.00	DAF RS200	8.65	218	ZF 4HP500	4 A
SB3000WS	RV	12.0	5.98	DAF WS242	11.6	329	ZF 8S-140	8 M
DENNIS (UK)								
Dart	RV	8.5	3.78	Cummins B	5.9	130	Allison AT545	4 A
Dart	RV	9.0	4.30	Cummins B	5.9	130	Allison AT545	4 A
Dart	RV	9.8	5.12	Cummins B	5.9	130	Allison AT545	4 A
Dart SLF	RV	9.0	4.40	Cummins B	5.9	130	Allison AT545	4 A
Dart SLF	RV	10.0	5.20	Cummins B	5.9	130	Allison AT545	4 A
Dart SLF	RV	10.5	5.81	Cummins B	5.9	145	Allison AT545	4 A
Javelin	UV	8.5	4.00	Cummins C	8.3	211	ZF S6-85	6 M
Javelin	UV	10.0	5.00	Cummins C	8.3	245	ZF S6-85	6 M
Javelin	UV	11.0	5.64	Cummins C	8.3	245	ZF S6-85	6 M
Javelin	UV	12.0	6.25	Cummins C	8.3	245	ZF S6-85	6 M
Javelin GX	UV	12.0	6.25	Cummins C	8.3	290	ZF S6-85	6 M
Javelin bus	UV	10.0	4.99	Cummins C	8.3	211	ZF S6-90	6 M
Javelin bus	UV	11.0	5.64	Cummins C	8.3	211	ZF S6-90	6 M
Lance	RV	10.5	5.05	Cummins C	8.3	211	ZF 4HP500	4 A
Lance	RV	11.0	5.85	Cummins C	8.3	211	ZF 4HP500	4 A
Lance	RV	11.5	5.85	Cummins C	8.3	211	ZF 4HP500	4 A
Lance SLF	RV	11.0	5.95	Cummins C	8.3	211	ZF 4HP500	4 A
Lance SLF	RV	11.5	5.95	Cummins C	8.3	211	ZF 4HP500	4 A
Lance dd	RV	10.5	5.05	Cummins C	8.3	215	ZF 4HP500	4 A
Dominator	RV	9.5	4.95	Cummins L10	10.0	215	ZF 4HP500	4 A
IVECO (Italy/Spain)								
DailyBus 49.10	FV	6.36	3.60	Iveco 8140.27S	2.5	104	Iveco 2826	5 M
DailyBus 49.10	FV	6.76	3.95	Iveco 8140.27S	2.5	104	Iveco 2826	5 M
DailyBus 59.12	FV	7.04	4.18	Iveco 8140.47S	2.5	116	Iveco 2826	5 M
DailyBus 59.12	FV	7.64	4.48	Iveco 8140.47S	2.5	116	Iveco 2826	5 M
EuroMidi	FV	9.73	4.63	Iveco 8060.45B	5.86	177	Iveco 2855.6	6 M
EuroRider	RV	12.0	6.15	Iveco 8060.41R	9.5	290	ZF S6-85	6 M
EuroRider	RV	12.0	6.15	Iveco 8060.41S	9.5	345	ZF 8S-180	8 M
TurboCity 50	RV	10.7	5.11	Iveco 8060.21	9.5	210	ZF 4HP500	4 A
KASSBOHRER integrals (Germany)								
Setra S250	RV	12.0	6.08	Mercedes OM442	15.1	296	ZF S6-90	6 M
Setra S250	RV	12.0	6.08	MAN D2866	12.0	370	ZF 8S-180	8 M
MAN (Germany)								
11.190 bus	RV	10.0	4.9	MAN D0826	6.9	190	ZF 4HP500	4 A
11.190 coach	RV	9.0	4.2	MAN D0826	6.9	190	ZF S6-36	6 M
11.220 bus	RV	10.0	4.9	MAN D0826	6.9	220	ZF 4HP500	4 A
18.370	RV	12.0	–	MAN D2866	12.0	370	ZF 8S-180	8 M
MARSHALL integrals (UK)								
Minibus	RV	8.5	3.94	Cummins B	3.9	135	Allison AT542	4 A
Minibus	RV	8.5	3.94	Perkins Phaser	4.0	135	Allison AT542	4 A

MERCEDES-BENZ (Germany)

Model	Engine pos.			Engine			Gearbox	
709D	FV	6.94	4.25	Mercedes OM364	3.97	86	Mercedes G2	5 M
711D	FV	6.94	4.25	Mercedes OM364A	3.97	105	Mercedes G2	5 M
811D	FV	7.49	4.80	Mercedes OM364A	3.97	105	Mercedes G2	5 M
814D	FV	7.49	4.80	Mercedes OM364A	3.97	135	Mercedes G3	6 M
OH1416	RV	11.3	5.70	Mercedes OM366A	5.96	165	Allison MT643	4 A
O405	RH	11.6	5.88	Mercedes OM447H	11.97	213	ZF 4HP500	4 A

NEOPLAN integral (Germany)

Model	Engine pos.			Engine			Gearbox	
N4009	RH	9.0	4.50	MAN D0824	10.0	155	Voith Midimat	4 A
N4014	RH	12.0	6.02	MAN D2866	12.0	230	ZF 5HP500	5 A
Jetliner N212H	RV	9.9	4.75	Mercedes OM401LA	9.6	290	ZF S6-85	6 M
Cityliner N116	RV	12.0	6.00	MAN D2866	12.0	370	ZF 8S-180	8 M
Cityliner N116	RV	12.0	6.00	Mercedes OM402LA	12.76	370	ZF 8S-180	8 M
Skyliner dd	RV	12.0	5.63	Mercedes OM442A	15.1	381	Allison B300R	4 A

OPTARE integrals (UK)

Model	Engine pos.			Engine			Gearbox	
MetroRider	FV	7.7	4.75	Cummins B	5.9	115	Allison AT545	4 A
MetroRider	FV	8.4	4.75	Cummins B	5.9	115	Allison AT545	4 A
Excel L960	RV	9.6	4.23	Cummins B	5.9	160	Allison B300R	4 A
Excel L1000	RV	10.0	4.66	Cummins B	5.9	160	Allison B300R	4 A
Excel L1070	RV	10.7	5.37	Cummins B	5.9	160	Allison B300R	4 A
Excel L1150	RV	11.5	6.09	Cummins B	5.9	160	Allison B300R	4 A

SCANIA (Sweden)

Model	Engine pos.			Engine			Gearbox	
FlexCi L113CRL	RV	11.7	5.90	Scania DSC11	11.0	230	ZF 4HP500	4 A
FlexCi L113CRL	RV	11.7	5.90	Scania DSC11	11.0	256	ZF 4HP500	4 A
MaxCi N113CRL	RV	11.36	6.00	Scania DSC11	11.0	230	Voith D863	3 A
N113DRB	RV	9.49	4.95	Scania DS11	11.0	220	Voith D863	3 A
N113DRB	RV	10.18	5.64	Scania DS11	11.0	220	Voith D863	3 A
K93CRB	RV	12.0	–	Scania DSC09	9.0	283	Scania GR801/CS	7 M
K113CRB	RV	12.0	–	Scania DSC11	11.0	320	Scania GR801/CS	7 M
K113TRB	RV	12.0	–	Scania DSC11	11.0	362	Scania GR801/CS	7 M

SPARTAN (USA)

Model	Engine pos.			Engine			Gearbox	
TX	RV	11.5	5.9	Cummins B	5.9	210	Allison AT545	4 A

VAN HOOL integrals (Belgium)

Model	Engine pos.			Engine			Gearbox	
T815	RV	12.0	6.00	MAN D2866	12.0	311	ZF S6-90	6 M
T815	RV	12.0	6.00	Cummins L10	10.0	290	ZF S6-90	6 M
EOS 80	RV	10.0	4.49	Mercedes OM401LA	9.6	290	ZF S6-85	6 M
EOS 90	RV	12.0	5.95	MAN D2866	12.0	311	ZF S6-85	6 M

VOLVO (Sweden/UK)

Model	Engine pos.			Engine			Gearbox	
Olympian	RV	9.6	4.95	Volvo D10A	9.6	245	ZF 4HP500	4 A
Olympian	RV	9.6	4.95	Cummins L10	10.0	215	ZF 4HP 500	4 A
Olympian	RV	10.3	6.64	Volvo D10A	9.6	245	ZF 4HP500	4 A
Olympian	RV	10.3	6.64	Cummins L10	10.0	215	ZF 4HP 500	4 A
B6	RV	8.5	3.61	Volvo D6A	5.48	180	ZF 4HP500	4 A
B6	RV	9.0	4.10	Volvo D6A	5.48	180	ZF 4HP500	4 A
B6	RV	9.9	5.00	Volvo D6A	5.48	180	ZF 4HP500	4 A
B6LE	RV	9.8	4.50	Volvo D6A	5.48	180	ZF 4HP500	4 A
B6LE	RV	10.6	5.32	Volvo D6A	5.48	180	ZF 4HP500	4 A
B6 coach	RV	9.0	4.50	Volvo D6A	5.48	180	ZF S6-36	6 M
B10B	RH	11.5	5.80	Volvo DH10A	9.6	245	ZF 4HP 500	4 A
B10L	RH	12.0	6.00	Volvo DH10A	9.6	245	ZF 4HP500	4 A
B10M	UH	12.0	6.20	Volvo DH10A	9.6	245	ZF S6-85	6 M
B10M	UH	12.0	6.20	Volvo DH10A	9.6	285	ZF S6-85	6 M
B10M	UH	12.0	6.20	Volvo DH10A	9.6	360	ZF S6-85	6 M
B10M SE	UH	12.0	6.65	Volvo DH10A	9.6	285	ZF S6-85	6 M
B10MT	UH	12.0	5.20	Volvo DH10A	9.6	360	Volvo G8 EGS	8 M
B12T	RV	12.0	6.10	Volvo D12A	12.0	380	Volvo G8 EGS	8 M

CODES: Engine position – **F** Front   Gearbox – number indicates forward speeds
U Underfloor   **A** Automatic
R Rear   **M** Manual
H Horizontal
V Vertical

More change at British Bus

BRITISH BUS expanded in 1995, with two significant takeovers during the year. There were also changes at a number of its existing operations.

The year started with the creation of a new company, Londonlinks Buses. This took over part of London & Country's operations, primarily in London, with operations from three depots - Croydon, Walworth and Dunton Green. It started life with a fleet of 162 buses acquired from London & Country and adopted a modified version of London & Country's two-tone green and red livery, with the most noticeable change being the adoption of light green rather than dark green for the roof.

A rather less significant change was the takeover in January of the 11-bus operation of District Bus of Wickford in Essex. This was initially put under the control of Southend Transport and then of London & Country, before being sold in the summer to FirstBus and absorbed by its Thamesway fleet.

The north west saw British Bus flexing its muscles in Warrington, with the launch in January by North Western of its Warrington Goldlines operation, using a fleet of 31 new Dennis Darts with Plaxton Pointer bodies. These had been stock vehicles and entered service in factory white. This was a direct attack on the operations of Warrington Borough Transport and WBT complained that the Goldlines name picked up on its own Midilines and Coachlines scheme. The Warrington bus war continued throughout 1995, and WBT responded by introducing new out-of-town routes to compete with established North Western services. North Western's aggression in Warrington was in sharp contrast to events in Liverpool where it had agreed to rationalise services with MTL.

In February North Western took over the services in the Leigh and Wigan areas which had been run by Heatons of Leigh. This followed the revocation of Heatons' operating licence. Six

Dennis Darts were added to a number of British Bus fleets. North Western received substantial numbers with bodies by Plaxton and East Lancs. Some of the East Lancs-bodied Darts introduced a new red, yellow and blue Cityplus livery to services in Liverpool. The colours were later adopted as a fleet standard.
Michael Fowler

routes were involved and a new brand name - Leigh Line - was adopted as the operation was put under the control of Bee Line. Leyland Nationals were used on the Leigh Line routes.

In March came the first of two major takeovers by British Bus, with the acquisition of Caldaire Holdings. Caldaire ran 400 vehicles and these pushed the British Bus fleet to the 5,000 mark, making it - briefly - number two to Stagecoach.

Caldaire had been a management buy-out from NBC of the West Riding group of companies, back in 1987. When British Bus took over there were four operating subsidiaries - West Riding, Yorkshire Woollen (which traded as Yorkshire Buses), Selby & District and South Yorkshire Transport. The last-named was an old-established independent based in Pontefract which had been bought by Caldaire in July 1994. The first sign of British Bus ownership was a revision of the livery layout used by the Caldaire companies, which did away with the upswept band of colour at the front of its vehicles.

The Caldaire takeover was quickly followed by another -

Maidstone & District. Like Caldaire, M&D was a former NBC operation which had been bought by its management, in the autumn of 1986. It ran 300 buses in an area adjoining that served by Kentish Bus, another British Bus subsidiary. This strengthened the position of the British Bus group in the area around London with its ownership sweeping right round the capital from Kent via Londonlinks, London & Country, Guildford & West Surrey and Luton & District which, of course, incorporated the former London Country North West business.

Changes were afoot at Luton & District in the summer. The ex-LCNW operations were running in the green and grey livery which had been in use when Luton & District took over in 1990. Buses used on the original Luton & District operations were red and cream, applied in the same style as the ex-LCNW vehicles. This was all swept aside in May, when the company was renamed LDT and started trading under the umbrella name of The Shires. The change was dramatic. An attractive new Best Impressions-designed livery - blue, yellow and grey - replaced the two existing schemes, and new local fleetnames were used for each area of operation, as shown in the accompanying list.

The Shires expanded too. In May it took over the bulk of the bus operations of Buffalo of Flitwick with a mixed fleet which included a number of modern types, including a Volvo B10B with Alexander Strider body, an uncommon type in a small fleet. The red and yellow Buffalo livery was replaced by The Shires' new scheme. The Buffalo bus service takeover was followed in July with the acquisition of the 17-strong bus fleet run by Motts of Aylesbury, trading as Yellow Buses (which gives a clue to the livery). Motts, like Buffalo, retained its coaching business. Motts had been running local buses since 1991 and had routes running into Oxford.

In the Midlands the small Frontline operation which ran in Tamworth and south to Birmingham was acquired from FirstBus by British Bus in the summer. It had been owned by Badgerline. It was put under the control of Stevensons.

There were further changes in the north west. Rationalisation in the Rochdale and Oldham areas saw Bee Line giving up services which had been competing with GM Buses North, while GMBN cut back in favour of Bee Line in the Leigh and Wigan areas. In May the operations of Star Line of Knutsford were acquired by British Bus. Star Line - the trading name for Arrowline - ran 45 buses, all but two of which were bought new. Most were Mercedes minis, but there were also Dennis Darts in the fleet. This takeover was referred to the Monopolies and Mergers Commission.

September saw British Bus take over two small post-deregulation operators. The first was Little White Buses of Ormskirk, which ran 13 minibuses in Skelmersdale and was acquired by North Western. These

were mainly Dodge S56s and Mercedes 811Ds, but included two Ivecos which were new in March. Little White Bus had started its services in 1987. Then came the Wigan Bus Company, which had only been running since 1992. The company had 12 buses, including one new Northern Counties-bodied DAF DB250 delivered not long before it sold-out to Bee Line. The DAF was the company's only double-decker.

Luton & District was not the only British Bus subsidiary with a new look in 1995. In the middle of the year Midland Red North abandoned its all-over red retro livery which hadn't really worked very well and effectively reverted to the previous yellow and red scheme. And Derby City Transport introduced a red, yellow and blue livery with City Rider fleetnames on certain busy routes - possibly inspired by the success of Trent's Spondon Flyer branding. It is to be extended to the entire Derby fleet.

In Liverpool North Western's operations were brightened up with the introduction of Cityplus services, where the company's red and blue livery was transformed by the addition of yellow on a fleet of new East Lancs-bodied Dennis Darts. The use of yellow relief was subsequently extended to other vehicles in the North Western fleet, brightening them up considerably.

In Scotland Clydeside 2000 was

renamed Clydeside Buses and the livery was standardised on a variant of the red, yellow and white scheme which had first appeared on new buses delivered in 1994 shortly before the company was acquired by British Bus. And there were changes at Kentish Bus, with the adoption of a yellow and green livery for services operated outside London. This happened in the autumn as Kentish Bus, Londonlinks Buses and Maidstone & District were linked with common management under the Invictaway umbrella, based in Maidstone - at what had been the Maidstone Borough Transport offices. As this was happening the neighbouring London & Country operation was falling foul of the traffic commissioner - and had its O-licence vehicle authorisation cut from 250 to 200 buses after concern had been expressed about maintenance standards.

New vehicles were delivered to most British Bus subsidiaries during 1995. Double-deckers were East Lancs-bodied Scanias for Derby City Transport and Midland Red North. Northumbria ordered 13 N113s with East Lancs' new Cityzen body, the first of which was exhibited at Coach & Bus 95.

Single-deckers were primarily Dennis Darts with sizeable numbers going to North Western (partly because of its Warrington expansion) and smaller numbers to

ECONOMY TRIALS

British Bus carried out fuel trials of an assortment of vehicle types at MIRA during the summer. Results, in descending order of economy, were

Model	Engine	Gearbox	mpg
Mercedes-Benz 811D	Mercedes OM364A	Allison AT545	14.9
Optare MetroRider	Cummins B	Allison AT545	14.1
MAN 11.190	MAN	ZF 4HP500	13.9
Dennis Dart	Cummins B	Allison AT545	13.1
Scania L113	Scania DSC11	ZF 4HP500	12.6
DAF SB220	DAF 1160	ZF 5HP500	10.9
Volvo B10B	Volvo THD103	ZF 4HP500	10.8
Volvo B6	Volvo TD63E	ZF 4HP500	10.6
Leyland National	Cummins B	Allison MT643	10.6
DAF DB250	DAF RS200	ZF 5HP500	10.3
Volvo Olympian	Cummins L10	ZF 4HP500	10.1
Scania N113	Scania DS11	Voith D863	7.8

The MAN 11.190 produced good figures for a bus of its size (which MAN was quick to use in its advertising), as did the Scania L113.

London & Country and Londonlinks. The group took 20 Plaxton-bodied Lances, divided equally between North Western and Clydeside 2000. The latter had a considerable injection of new single-deck buses at the start of the year, including Scanias with bodywork by Alexander, East Lancs and Northern Counties (the mixture pointing to the purchase of stock vehicles to speed delivery) and Plaxton-bodied Dennis Darts. Four MANs with Optare Vecta bodies were bought by Crosville Wales.

An order for 100 Scanias was announced during the year and these included L113s with East Lancs bodies for Northumbria and The Shires, and with Wright bodies for Kentish Bus. London & Country also placed orders for new Dennises for 1996 - 25 Lances (including 10 of the new double-deck version) and four Dominators. Notable second-hand purchases by London & Country were the three Dennis Dominators purchased by Mayne of Manchester in 1993 which had originally been intended for Strathclyde Buses. They moved south at the end of the year.

Minibuses for the group were mainly Mercedes with bodies by Plaxton (for The Shires) and Alexander for Bee Line, Crosville Wales, Midland Fox and Midland Red North. The last-named got two batches - the first in the old livery, the second in the new. Optare MetroRiders were delivered to London & Country and Northumbria.

In December British Bus announced its orders for 1996-97, comprising 533 buses. Most are Dennis Dart SLFs - 224 in all -but there will also be 73 Scania single-deckers, 65 Volvo Olympians, 126 Mercedes 709Ds and 45 Optare MetroRiders. Bodywork will be supplied by Alexander, East Lancs, Northern Counties and Plaxton. Northern Counties bodies will be fitted to all the double-deckers, while some of the Darts are likely to have the first examples of East Lancs' new Alusuisse midibus body.

By the end of 1995 British Bus was running around 5,000 vehicles - putting it in third place behind Stagecoach and FirstBus.

THE BRITISH BUS GROUP

Bee Line Buzz Co	Maidstone & District
Clydeside Buses	New Enterprise
Colchester Borough Transport	Midland Fox
Crosville Wales	Fairtax Foxhound
Derby City Transport	Fox Cab
Blue Bus	Fox Cub
City Rider	Midland Red North
Gem Fairtax	North Western Road Car
Guildford	Arrowline
& West Surrey Buses	Star Line
Horsham Buses	Warrington Goldlines
Kentish Bus & Coach Co	Northumbria Motor Services
LDT - The Shires	Hunters
Aylesbury & The Vale	Southend Transport
Chiltern Rover	Stevensons
Gade Valley	Frontline (Tamworth)
Hitchin & District	Viking
Luton & Dunstable	Yorkshire Bus Group
Network Watford	Selby & District
Stevenage Line	South Yorkshire
Stuart Palmer	Road Transport
Liverline Travel	West Riding Automobile Co
London & Country	Yorkshire Woollen District
Londonlinks Buses	Yorkshire Buses

Luton & District underwent a transformation in 1995, emerging as The Shires with a new livery and new fleetnames. Among the first new buses to be supplied in the new colours were 33 Plaxton-bodied Mercedes minibuses.

Kentish Bus introduced low-floor buses to a service in the Dartford area. These were Scania Axcess-ultralows, bodied by Wright of Ballymena which has made something of a speciality in the provision of accessible buses. They carried the new green and yellow livery being used on Kentish Bus operations outside London.

A decade of Optare

An artist's impression of the Optare Excel was released prior to the vehicle's launch in October. The real thing can be seen on page 12.

TEN YEARS AGO Britain's bus manufacturing was in crisis. And at the centre of the turmoil was Leyland. Leyland was not only Britain's biggest chassis maker; it was the country's biggest bodybuilder too, with two busy and old-established factories - Eastern Coach Works at Lowestoft and Charles H Roe at Leeds.

The Roe factory was axed in 1985 - and then to everyone's surprise found a new lease of life under new ownership. Optare had arrived. Its first products were pretty unexciting. It built some Roe-style double-deck bodies on Olympians for Cambus, Maidstone Boro'line, Reading Transport and the West Yorkshire PTE. And it produced some neat but boxy midibuses on front-engined Leyland Cub and rear-engined Dennis Domino chassis.

There was no hint of the revolution to come.

The first new Optare product was the eye-catching CityPacer, based on a Volkswagen LT chassis. It was a radical approach to minibus design, a modern shape which concealed the light truck chassis beneath. And it also set the seal for future model policy, offering body designs which were built for a specific chassis and which were marketed as Optares, not as Optare-bodied Volkswagens or whatever.

The first CityPacers took to the streets in 1986. A bigger minibus, the StarRider, followed in 1987 on Mercedes-Benz chassis. It echoed the CityPacer theme, with the front

end being an integral part of the body rather than being built around the standard Mercedes snub-nosed bonnet - although that was offered as a cost-saving option.

A big bus appeared in 1988 - the Delta. This used the Alusuisse system of aluminium extrusions to produce the most stylish single-decker yet seen in Britain. It was based on the new DAF SB220 chassis.

Optare acquired the design rights for MCW's minibus, the Metrorider. This had been far from satisfactory in service, with a number of users pursuing legal action against MCW. It was extensively re-worked by Optare before being launched as an Optare product in 1989. The MetroRider is an integral with a Cummins engine and Optare have developed wider and longer versions - up to 8.4m - to cater for a broader range of operations. The MetroRider effectively replaced the CityPacer and the StarRider.

Optare had developed close links with DAF Bus, and in 1990 followed it in to the new United Bus

organisation. However United Bus lasted just four years and when it folded, largely as a result of the collapse of the Dutch market, Optare regained its independence.

A double-decker, the Spectra, was launched in 1991 and introduced DAF's DB250 chassis to the market. This was developed by DAF as a replacement for the Metrobus, following the closure of MCW in 1989 - although there is little of the original MCW design in the DAF-built product. The main Spectra users in Britain are Wilts & Dorset, Reading Transport and London Central.

Further new models have followed. The 10m Vecta, built on an MAN 11.190 chassis, was another 1991 launch and the bigger Sigma appeared in 1994, on the Dennis Lance. The main user of the Vecta is North East Bus, while the Sigma is in operation with the Go-Ahead Group and with Trent, a loyal Optare customer. In 1995 two new models appeared, the Mercedes-based Prisma (see page xx) and the low-floor Excel, an integral spanning a broad range of sizes from 9.6m to 11.5m (see page 12).

Optare has an involvement in the coach market too, through its Bova UK operation which imports the Dutch-built Futura integral.

The company's business is not restricted to the UK. It has sold Spectra double-deckers to Turkey, and currently has a major contract in hand for the supply of 1,200 MetroRiders to Malaysia.

1995 OPTARE PRODUCTS		
Model	**Chassis**	**Introduced**
Delta	DAF SB220	1988
MetroRider	integral	1989
Vecta	MAN 11.190	1991
Spectra	DAF DB250	1991
Sigma	Dennis Lance	1994
Prisma	Mercedes O405	1995
Excel	integral	1995

New in the Midlands

There were prior to 1995 few small buses in the Trent fleet. That changed during the year with the arrival of 26 Optare MetroRiders. Trent also runs bigger Optare models in the shape of Vectas, Sigmas and Deltas. *Michael Fowler*

There are few Alexander Striders in service with small companies. One, on a Volvo B10B chassis, was delivered to Felix of Ilkeston. It runs on the Ilkeston to Derby service alongside another unusual type for a small fleet, a Leyland Lynx II. *Stewart J Brown*

Nottingham City Transport added three types of Alexander-bodied Volvo single-deckers to its fleet in 1995. These were B6s with Dash bodies, B10Ms with PS-type bodies and, as shown here, nine Volvo B10Bs with Strider bodies. *Stewart J Brown*

Derby City Transport adopted a new livery and new fleetname - City Rider - in 1995. The first new buses to carry it were five Scania N113s with East Lancs bodies, which entered service in August. *Tony Wilson*

The Go-Ahead Group introduced new two-door Dennis Darts to its Oxford fleet in 1995. They had Marshall bodies. *Tim Carter*

New owners at Northern Counties

AFTER A FEW YEARS of uncertainty and change, Northern Counties found new security in 1995 as part of the Henlys Group. Henlys are the owners of Britain's biggest coachbuilder, Plaxton.

Northern Counties has a long history of bus body production, having been formed in 1919. It started building car bodies, but quickly moved on to buses. The business expanded during the 1920s and 1930s, and Northern Counties was one of the small number of bus body manufacturers which built utility bodywork during World War 2, mainly on Guy Arab chassis and including substantial numbers for London Transport.

The 1950s and 1960s saw the company supplying bodywork to operators throughout the country, including some in the nationalised SMT group - notably Central SMT and Western SMT - and to the BET group, including big fleets such as Southdown. It was also a supplier to a number of municipal and independent operators. It took over the competing Massey Bros business in 1967 and the site in Pemberton from which the company now operates is in fact the Massey site.

The creation of the Passenger Transport Executives from 1969 saw changes in bus buying patterns and Northern Counties soon became closely identified with its biggest customer - SELNEC and its successor, Greater Manchester Transport. Ultimately, in 1983, the PTE bought Northern Counties. This did not stop the company continuing to supply other operators.

Deregulation saw diversification into minibuses, mainly on Dodge chassis for GMT, but for a few other operators too. A minibus body with a streamlined front was devised for the Dodge (or Renault as it was then called),

entering production at the start of 1988, and developed in response to new-look minibuses coming from Optare and MCW. The links with Renault saw an attempt to market the full-size PR100 in the UK, with Northern Counties building bodywork to Renault's designs. It was not a success and just five were built, including three airside buses. The cut-backs in new bus purchasing which saw the demise of Leyland Bus and MCW had an effect on Northern Counties too, and the company went into administrative receivership in May 1991.

This did not halt the development of a new single-deck body, initially called the CountyBus and then rechristened Paladin. The double-decker was named the Palatine, and a stylish new double-deck body was launched in 1993 as the Palatine II. The single-deck evolved, with a stepped waistline model appearing on the Volvo B6 chassis, and with an improved front end being phased in on the Dart version from 1994. The minibus body was given the Pageant name, but production ceased in 1992 as orders for big buses started to pick up again.

Rescue came in August 1992 in the form of a management buy-out and the company continued to find new customers. It became a major supplier to companies in the London area - including both London Buses and some of the independents - and

has vied with Alexander for the position of the country's leading double-deck builder.

Major customers in the 1990s have included Bristol City Line, British Bus, Capital Citybus, CentreWest, East Kent, East Yorkshire, Kentish Bus, London Central, London General, Maidstone & District, Metroline, MTL, Southern Vectis, Stagecoach and Warrington Borough Transport.

The company was bought by Henlys in May. The Palatine double-deck models complement the range produced by Plaxton, but the Paladin competes with the Pointer and the Verde. The Pointer easily outsells Northern Counties' midibus version of the Paladin, but the full-size version is running just about level with Plaxton's Verde in terms of sales. The Paladin sells to Stagecoach; the Verde to FirstBus.

It seems reasonable to forecast that eventually the Pointer will be the only design offered by either of the two companies on low-floor midis, and that Northern Counties' new body on the SB220 will be the only offering on full-size low-floor buses -and that there will therefore be no low-floor Verde or Paladin. Rationalisation of the two companies' product ranges must surely be coming, but it may be that chassis choices and the strong swing towards low-floor buses will prove to be one of the major deciding factors in who ultimately builds what.

WHO BUILDS WHAT AT HENLYS			
Type	**Model**	**Built at**	**On**
Minibus	Plaxton Beaver	Anston	Mercedes T2
Midibus	Plaxton Pointer	Scarborough	Dart, B6
	NC Paladin	Wigan	Dart, B6
Low-floor midibus	Plaxton Pointer	Scarborough	Dart SLF, B6LE
Full-size sd	Plaxton Verde	Scarborough	Lance, B10B
	NC Paladin	Wigan	B10B, L113, SB220
Low-floor sd	NC	Wigan	SB220
Double-deck	NC Palatine	Wigan	DB250, Olympian, Lance
Coach	Plaxton Premiere	Scarborough	Javelin, B10M, SB3000
	Plaxton Excalibur	Scarborough	Javelin, B10M, B12T

Who owns whom...

A quick guide to the major groups and their key subsidiary companies, associated companies and principal trading names.

Blackpool Transport Services
Handybus
Fylde Transport
    Baby Blues
    Blue Buses
    Seagull Coaches

Blazefield Holdings
BTS Coaches
Cambridge Coach Services
    Rover Coaches
Harrogate & District Travel
Keighley & District Travel
    Northern Rose
Sovereign Bus & Coach Co
Sovereign Buses (Harrow)
Welwyn & Hatfield Line Bus Co
Yorkshire Coastliner

Bournemouth Transport
Christchurch Buses
Dorset Travel Services
Yellow Buses
Yellow Coaches

Brighton Transport
Brighton Blue Bus
Lewes Coaches

British Bus - see page 33

Burnley & Pendle Transport Co
Viscount Central
Whizzard

Cawlett group
North Devon
    Atlantic Blue
    Red Bus
    South Western
    Tiverton & District
Pearce, Darch & Willcox
    Comfy-Lux
Southern National
Taylors Coaches
West Dorset Coaches

Cowie Group
Grey-Green
Leaside Buses
South London Transport
Hughes DAF

Durham Travel Services
York Pullman

EYMS Group
East Yorkshire Motor Services
East Yorkshire Travel
    Teesside Coach Travel
Finglands
Hull & District
Primrose Valley Coaches
Scarborough & District Motor Services
Scarborough Skipper

FirstBus - see page 28

Go-Ahead Group
Brighton & Hove Bus and Coach Co
City of Oxford Motor Services
    The Oxford Bus Company
    The Wycombe Bus Company
Gateshead & District Omnibus Co
    Go-Ahead Gateshead
Langley Park Motor Co
    Gypsy Queen
London Central Bus Co
    Camberwell Clipper
Low Fell Coaches
Northern General Transport Co
Northern National Omnibus Co
OK Motor Services
Sunderland & District Omnibus Co
    Wear Buses
Tynemouth & District Omnibus Co
    Coastline
Tyneside Omnibus Co
    VFM Buses
Visitauto
    Metro Buses
Voyager

Great Yarmouth Transport
Blue Buses
Yareside Coaches

Hyndburn Transport
Rigbys

London General Transport Services
The Clapham Omnibus
Red Arrow
Streetline

London United
Airbus
Harrier
Hounslow Hoppa
Kingston Bus
Kingston Hoppa
Riverside Bus
Skipper
Southall Shuttle
Stanwell Buses
    Westlink

Lynton Travel Group
Airport Coaches
Biss Brothers Travel

Metroline group
Atlas Bus & Coach
Brents Travel
Metroline Travel
    Skipper

MTL Trust Holdings
Coach 2000
Fareway Passenger Services
Liverbus
Merseyrider
Merseyside Transport
    Lancashire Travel

    Merseybus
    Sightseers
    Southport & District
    Wirral Peninsula
MTL Heysham
MTL London Northern Bus Co
    Camden Link
    MTL London
    Red Express
    R&I

National Car Parks
Capital Coaches
Marton
Whytes

National Express Group
Eurolines
National Express
    Rapide
National Expressliners
Polski Express
Scottish Citylink
Speedlink Airport Services
    Flightline
    Jetlink

Northern Ireland Transport Holding Company
Citybus
Flexibus
Ulsterbus
    BusyBus
    Goldliner

Nottingham City Transport
South Notts

Pullmans
London Coaches
North Kent Road Car Co

Q Drive Buses
The Bee Line
Limebourne Coaches
London Buslines
AVE Berkhof

Rapson group
Highland Country Buses
Highland Scottish Omnibuses
Rapson Coaches

Reading Transport
Goldline Travel
London Line
Newbury Buses
Reading Buses

Rhondda Buses
Caerphilly Busways
Parfitts Motor Services

Rossendale Transport
Ellen Smith Coaches

SB Holdings
GCT

Kelvin Central Buses
    KCB Network
SB Travel
Strathclyde Buses

Southern Vectis
Musterphantom
    Solent Blue Line
Southern Vectis Omnibus Co

Stagecoach Holdings - see page 17

Taybus Holdings
Dundee Bus Co (not trading)
Tayside Public Transport Co
    Tayside Greyhound
Wishart (Friockheim)

Thamesdown Transport
Dartline
Green Bus
Kingston Coaches

Transit Holdings
Bayline
Blue Admiral
Devon General
Docklands Transit
Red Admiral
Thames Transit
    The Oxford Tube
    Blackbird Flyer
    Carousel
    Kidlington Cavalier
    Rose Hill Runners

Warrington Borough Transport
Coach Lines
Midi Lines

Wellglade
Barton Buses
Trent Motor Traction Co

West Midlands Travel Group
Central Coachways
County Bus & Coach Co
    Lea Valley
    ThameSide
    Town Link
North East Bus
    Tees & District Transport Co
    Teesside Motor Services
    United Automobile Services
        Eden Bus Services
Smiths Coaches (Shennington)
    Your Bus
West Midlands Travel
    WM Buses

Wilts & Dorset
Hants & Dorset Motor Services
    Damory Coaches
Tourist Coaches
Wilts & Dorset Bus Co

Yorkshire Traction Group
Andrews (Sheffield)
Barnsley & District Traction Co
Basichour
    Sheffield Omnibus
Lincolnshire Road Car Co
Meffan (Kirriemuir)
Strathtay Scottish
Tanport
    South Riding
Yorkshire Terrier
    Kingsman

Yorkshire Traction Co
    Coachlink
    County
    Fastlink
    Mexborough & Swinton
    Townlink

Henlys plc
Kirkby Coach & Bus
Northern Counties
Plaxton Coach & Bus
Prevost (Canada) (49 per cent)
Roadlease
    National Expressliners

Volvo Bus
Drogmoller
Prevost (Canada) (51 per cent)
Steyr
Yeates Bus & Coach

Before selling out to MTL, R&I adopted a modified livery featuring red for the front and lower side panels. New vehicles in the new livery included four Dennis Darts with Plaxton Pointer bodies. MTL is adopting all-over red for the R&I operation. *Stewart J Brown*

New
in the
South

Newport Transport is an old-established Scania user and added further examples of the Swedish marque to its fleet in 1995. These were N113s with Alexander Strider bodies.

Ikarus-bodied DAF SB220s are an unusual choice for a local authority fleet. Four were delivered to Eastbourne Buses in 1995.
Michael Fowler

A Dennis Lance SLF with Wright Pathfinder body demonstrates the extendable ramp designed to ease access for wheelchair users. It was one of 10 which were partially funded by Essex county council. Four each went to Southend Transport and County Bus & Coach, and two to Hedingham & District.

Brighton Transport added more Dennis Darts to its operations in 1995, taking eight with Plaxton Pointer bodies. It has low-floor versions on order for 1996. *Michael Fowler*

Two 10.6m-long Volvo B6LE accessible midibuses with Wright Crusader bodies were purchased by Ralphs Coaches of Langley for use on a contract linking Heathrow Airport with the Holiday Inn Crowne Plaza hotel. They were 35-seaters

The first Dennis Darts for Cardiff City Transport were delivered in 1995. They had Alexander Dash bodies.

Dennis - riding high in its centenary year

DENNIS CELEBRATED ITS centenary in 1995, a year in which bus output reached record levels as the company continued to win new customers for its Dart, Lance and Javelin models.

The company was founded by brothers John and Raymond Dennis in Guildford in 1895, initially building bicycles. The first motorised vehicle, a tricycle, was produced in 1898 and from the turn of the century the company started to grow rapidly, producing high-quality cars. Light commercial vehicles soon followed. The first bus was built in 1904 and the first fire engine followed four years later in 1908. Car production ceased in 1913 and the company concentrated on commercial vehicles. Lorries were an important part of the company's production during World War I - when over 7,000 were built - and for some years thereafter.

Peace returned in 1918, and bus production was resumed and continued throughout the 1920s and 1930s. When Greyhound of Bristol introduced what is claimed to be Britain's first long-distance express coach service to London in 1925 it did so with a fleet of Dennises. The first London bus to run on pneumatic tyres, also in 1925, was a Dennis single-decker in the Admiral fleet. In the following year Dennis was again in the lead with the first bus in London to have four-wheel brakes, again for Admiral.

The late 1920s saw Dennis selling buses to a number of municipal and company fleets. Amongst the biggest users were Nottingham and South Wales Transport, each with 76 Dennises in operation in the late 1920s. Colchester Corporation's first buses, in 1928, were Dennises.

The early models were known by type letters, but with the launch of a new generation of chassis from 1930 came names -some of which are still familiar more than 60 years

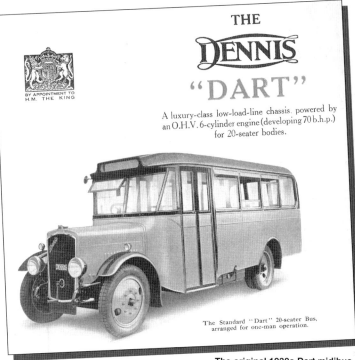

THE

DENNIS "DART"

A luxury-class low-load-line chassis, powered by an O.H.V. 6-cylinder engine (developing 70 b.h.p.) for 20-seater bodies.

The Standard "Dart" 20-seater Bus, arranged for one-man operation.

The original 1930s Dart midibus.

later. First came the double-deck Lance and the single-deck Arrow, which was quickly replaced by the lower cost Lancet. A trolleybus was catalogued, but none were built - at least not until 1984. There was also a bewildering variety of small buses, many of which were built in limited numbers - Ace, Dart, Arrow Minor, Pike, Falcon.

The postwar Lance double-decker sold in small numbers, but the equivalent Lancet single-deck chassis was widely used by coach operators in the late 1940s. In 1949 production hit a postwar peak as the company built 1,096 buses and trucks. Underfloor-engined chassis were built in small numbers in the 1950s, and double-deck sales were given a new lease of life in the late 1950s and early 1960s with the low-frame Loline, a Bristol Lodekka built under licence.

But the company was in decline. It ceased engine manufacture in 1961. The Loline -

now the company's only bus model - sold in smallish numbers until 1967 and at that point Dennis decided to concentrate its resources on trucks and fire appliances. Bus production halted. However Dennis was still struggling and in 1972 came a change of ownership when the company was bought by the Hestair group.

Hestair invested in new models for the fire and municipal markets. Then it turned its attention to buses, an area in which by this time British Leyland effectively had a monopoly. This led to a bus renaissance, with the appearance in 1977 of the new Gardner-engined Dominator. Further models followed - Jubilant, Falcon, Lancet, Dragon, Condor, Dorchester and Domino. A trolleybus was built for trial by the South Yorkshire PTE in 1984 - Dennis's first.

The latter part of the 1980s saw yet more new model development. The Javelin coach chassis was launched in 1986. Then came the most successful bus chassis in the company's history: the Dart. It was unveiled in 1989. By the end of 1995 over 3,000 had been built for service in Britain and abroad. The simple engineering philosophy which made the midi-sized Dart a success was then applied to a big single-deck chassis, the Lance, and both models were subsequently developed with low floors - the SLF, Super Low Floor, variants. The Lance has also been engineered as a double-decker, and in this form was first exhibited at Coach & Bus 95. All of these new models use Cummins engines.

The company's expansion has since 1989 been under the control of Trinity Holdings, a management buy-out from Hestair. A new factory was built on a greenfield site in Guildford and opened in 1990. The 1990s have seen output and sales rise steadily and in its centenary year Dennis built no fewer than 1,685 vehicles - buses, coaches and fire appliances - at its Guildford factory. In addition it exported a significant number of bus and coach chassis kits to Malaysia for local assembly.

It also produced Britain's first purpose-built bus designed to run on compressed natural gas, a Dart with Plaxton Pointer bodywork which was scheduled to enter service in Bristol at the start of 1996 with FirstBus subsidiary Bristol City Line.

When Dennis re-entered the psv market in 1977 it was facing up to Leyland, selling Atlanteans, Fleetlines, VRTs and Nationals - and with the new high-tech Titan in the offing. Volvo was selling the Ailsa, and MCW's Metrobus was about to be launched. Ford and Bedford were leading lights in the coach market. Who would have forecast then that Dennis would still be selling buses and coaches almost 20 years later, and that Ford, Bedford, MCW and even the mighty Leyland would all have been consigned to history?

New buses for the Wigan Bus Company in 1995 included three Dennis Darts with Northern Counties bodies. The company sold out to British Bus in September.
Stewart J Brown

The first Dennis Lance double-decker - since the 1950s at any rate - was this smart bus with Northern Counties Palatine II body. It is one of a pair for Nottingham City Transport.
Stewart J Brown

CENTENARY

DENNIS

· 1895 - 1995 ·

THE 1995 DENNIS RANGE		
Model	**Application**	**Launched**
Dominator	Double-deck bus	1977
Condor	Export double-deck	1980
Javelin	Mid-engined coach	1986
Dart	Midibus	1989
Lance	Single-deck city bus	1990
Lance SLF	Low-floor city bus	1993
Dart SLF	Low-floor midibus	1995
Lance	Double-deck bus	1995

1995 deliveries

Key deliveries to significant operators in 1995

AA, Troon	1 DAF SB220/Northern Counties
	3 Dennis Dart/Northern Counties
	8 Mercedes T2/Alexander Sprint
ABC, Formby	3 Optare MetroRider
Ashton, Port Glasgow	9 Mercedes T2/WS Coachbuilders
	1 Mercedes OH1416/Wright Urbanranger
Badgerline Ltd	15 Dennis Dart/Plaxton Pointer
	5 Dennis Lance SLF/Wright Pathfinder
	7 Dennis Javelin/Plaxton Premiere
Barnsley & District	3 Volvo B6/Alexander Dash
Bebb, Llantwit Fardre	16 Volvo B10M/Plaxton
Bee Line, Warminster	7 Mercedes T2/Plaxton Beaver
Black Prince, Leeds	4 MAN 11.190/Optare Vecta
Blackburn Transport	6 Optare MetroRider
Blackpool Transport	8 Optare MetroRider
Blue Bus, Horwich	1 Dennis Dart/Plaxton Pointer
	2 Dennis Dart/Alexander Dash
Bluebird, Middleton	6 Iveco 59.12/Marshall
	3 Iveco 59.12/Mellor
Bournemouth Transport	12 Dennis Dart/East Lancs
Brewer, Port Talbot	10 Dennis Dart/Plaxton Pointer
Brighton Transport	8 Dennis Dart/Plaxton Pointer
Brighton & Hove	20 Dennis Dart/Marshall
Bristol Cityline	40 Dennis Dart/Plaxton Pointer
	32 Mercedes T2/Plaxton Beaver
British Airways	29 Van Hool A308/Van Hool
	33 Mercedes T2/Wright NimBus
Bullock, Cheadle	4 Scania L113/Wright Axcess-ultralow
	2 Volvo Olympian East Lancs
Bus Eireann	10 Volvo B10M/Plaxton Premiere
Cambus	3 Volvo Olympian/Northern Counties
	4 Optare MetroRider
Canavan, Kilsyth	2 Dennis Dart/Plaxton Pointer
Cardiff Bluebird	2 Dennis Dart/Plaxton Pointer
Cardiff City Transport	17 Optare MetroRider
	7 Dennis Dart/Alexander Dash
Castleways, Winchcombe	1 Dennis Dart/Plaxton Pointer
Catch-A-Bus, East Boldon	3 Dennis Dart/Plaxton Pointer
CentreWest	32 Dennis Dart/Plaxton Pointer
	12 Volvo Olympian/Northern Counties
	7 Mercedes T2/Marshall
Chambers, Bures	1 Volvo Olympian/Northern Counties
Citibus, Manchester	7 Iveco 59.12/Marshall
City of Oxford	20 Dennis Dart/Marshall
	28 Dennis Lance/Plaxton Verde (z)
Clarke, London	12 Volvo B10M/Jonckheere
	2 Volvo B12T/Jonckheere Monaco
Clarkson, South Elmsall	2 DAF SB220/Ikarus Citibus
Clydeside Buses	2 Scania L113/Northern Counties
	4 Scania L113/Alexander Strider
	8 Scania L113/East Lancs
	3 Scania MaxCi/East Lancs
	2 Dennis Dart/Plaxton Pointer
	10 Dennis Lance/Plaxton Verde
CMT, Liverpool	4 Volvo B10B/Wright Endurance
	7 Dennis Dart/Northern Counties
Coastline, North Shields	5 Optare MetroRider
County Bus & Coach	15 Iveco 59.12/Marshall
Crosville Wales	4 MAN 11.190/Optare Vecta
	8 Mercedes T2/Alexander Sprint
Davies, Pencader	1 Dennis Dart/East Lancs
de Courcey, Coventry	2 Iveco TurboCity 50/WS Coachbuilders
Delaine, Bourne	3 Volvo Olympian/East Lancs
Delta, Mansfield	1 Dennis Dart/Marshall
	4 DAF SB220/Northern Counties
Derby City Transport	5 Scania N113/East Lancs dd
Devon General	25 Mercedes T2/Marshall
Dublin Bus	30 DAF SB220/Alexander Setanta (a)
	80 Volvo Olympian/Alexander R
East London	27 Dennis Dart/Alexander Dash
East Sussex CC	2 Dennis Dart/LCB
East Yorkshire	6 Volvo Olympian/Northern Counties
	14 Volvo Olympian/Alexander Royale
Eastbourne Buses	4 DAF SB220/Ikarus Citibus
Eastern Counties	8 Dennis Dart/Plaxton Pointer
	2 Mercedes T2/Alexander Sprint
	15 Mercedes T2/Frank Guy
Eastern National	8 Dennis Dart/Plaxton Pointer
	20 Dennis Dart/Plaxton Beaver
Eastern Scottish	10 Mercedes O405/Optare Prisma
Epsom Buses	2 Dennis Dart/Plaxton Pointer
Excelsior, Bournemouth	23 Volvo B10M/Plaxton
	2 Volvo B12T/Jonckheere Monaco
Felix, Stanley	1 Volvo B10B/Alexander Strider
Finglands, Manchester	4 Volvo Olympian/Alexander Royale
Fowlers, Holbeach Grove	3 Scania L113/Northern Counties
Galloway, Mendlesham	1 DAF SB220/Ikarus Citibus
GM Buses North	20 Volvo B10B/Wright Endurance
	35 Volvo B10B/Wright Endurance (z)
	10 Volvo B6/Northern Counties
	18 Dennis Dart/Northern Counties
	1 Volvo B6LE/Wright Crusader
GM Buses South	30 Mercedes T2/Alexander Sprint
Go-Ahead Gateshead	5 DAF SB220/Optare Delta
Godson, Leeds	2 DAF SB220/Ikarus Citibus
Grampian Transport	10 Mercedes O405/Optare Prisma
	6 Dennis Dart/Alexander Dash (c,z)
Grey-Green, London	3 Scania N113/Northern Counties
	2 Dennis Dart/Plaxton Pointer
Hallmark, Luton	3 DAF SB220/Ikarus Citibus
Halton Transport	9 Dennis Dart/Marshall
Harrogate & District	5 Volvo B10B/Alexander Strider
	4 Volvo B6/Alexander Dash
Hedingham & District	2 Dennis Lance SLF/Wright Pathfinder
Highland Scottish	2 Mercedes 811D/Alexander Sprint
Hong Kong Citybus	40 Leyland Olympian/Alexander R
	50 Dennis Dragon/Duple Metsec/Caetano
	21 Dennis Dart/Plaxton Pointer
Hutchison, Overtown	2 MAN 11.190/Optare Vecta
Ipswich Buses	3 Volvo Olympian/East Lancs
Islwyn Borough Transport	3 Mercedes 811D/Plaxton Beaver
JMT, Jersey	5 Dennis Dart/Plaxton Pointer
Jones, Rhos	1 Dennis Dart/Plaxton Pointer
Kentish Bus	10 Scania L113/Wright Axcess-ultralow
Kelvin Central	16 Volvo Olympian/Alexander Royale
	60 Volvo B10M/Alexander PS (z)
KMB, Hong Kong	10 Scania N113 3-axle
Lamberts, Beccles	2 Volvo B6/Plaxton Pointer
Leaside Buses	14 Dennis Dart/Plaxton Pointer
	13 DAF DB250/Northern Counties
Leicester Citybus	10 Mercedes O405/Optare Prisma
Leon, Finningley	2 Optare MetroRider
Lincolnshire Road Car	8 Volvo B6/East Lancs
Liverbus	4 Volvo B10B/Northern Counties (a)
London Central	9 Volvo Olympian/Alexander Royale
	27 Volvo Olympian/Northern Counties
London General	16 Dennis Dart/Plaxton Pointer
	1 Volvo B6LE/Wright Crusader
London United	12 Volvo Olympian/Alexander Royale
London & Country	14 Optare/MetroRider
	8 Dennis Dart/East Lancs
	6 Dennis Lance SLF/Wright Pathfinder
	3 Mercedes T2/Alexander Sprint
Londonlinks	4 Dennis Dart/Plaxton Pointer
Lothian	33 Volvo Olympian/Alexander
	2 Dennis Javelin/Caetano Algarve II

46

Lowland	2	Scania L113/Wright (d)
Lucketts, Watford	1	Iveco TurboCity/WS Coachbuilders
Maidstone & District	5	Volvo Olympian/Northern Counties
	9	Volvo B6/Plaxton Pointer
Mainline	30	Volvo B6/Plaxton Pointer
	25	Volvo B10M/Alexander PS
	11	Volvo B6LE/Wright Crusader
Manchester Airport	6	Dennis Dart/Marshall
Mayne, Manchester	2	Scania N113/East Lancs dd
McGill, Barrhead	4	Dennis Dart/Northern Counties
Mercury, Rochester	1	Dennis Dart/Marshall
Metrobus, Orpington	6	Dennis Dart/Plaxton Pointer
Midland Bluebird	8	Scania L113/Wright
	5	Mercedes T2/Alexander Sprint
	1	Optare MetroRider
Midland Choice	2	Dennis Dart/Northern Counties
	2	Mercedes OH1416/Wright Urbanranger
Midland Fox	12	Mercedes T2/Alexander Sprint
Midland Red North	21	Mercedes T2/Alexander Sprint
	4	Scania MaxCi/East Lancs
	5	Scania N113/East Lancs dd
	3	Dennis Dart/Marshall
MTL	3	Neoplan N4009/Neoplan
Myall, Bassingbourn	1	Volvo B6/Alexander Dash
NCP, Birmingham Airport	2	Dennis Dart/Plaxton Pointer
Newport Transport	6	Scania N113/Alexander Strider
North Western	10	Dennis Lance/Plaxton Verde
	29	Dennis Dart/Plaxton Pointer
	58	Dennis Dart/East Lancs
Northampton Transport	3	Volvo B10L/Alexander Ultra
Northumbria	18	Optare MetroRider
	10	Scania L113/East Lancs
Nottingham City Transport	9	Volvo B10B/Wright Endurance
	9	Volvo B10B/Alexander Strider
	2	Volvo B10B/Plaxton Verde
	5	Volvo B10M/Alexander PS
	2	Dennis Lance/Northern Counties dd (z)
	5	Scania L113/Wright/Axcess-ultralow (z)
	10	Mercedes T2/Plaxton Beaver
	3	Mercedes T2/Alexander Sprint
	3	Volvo B6/Alexander Dash
Parfitts	2	Dennis Dart/Plaxton Pointer
Park, Hamilton	42	Volvo B10M/Van Hool Alizee
	27	Volvo B10M/Jonckheere
	5	Volvo B12/Van Hool dd
Plymouth Citybus	15	Mercedes T2/Plaxton Beaver
PMT	21	Mercedes T2/Plaxton Beaver
	5	Dennis Lance/Plaxton Verde
Preston Bus	14	Optare MetroRider
Pride of the Road	6	DAF SB220/Ikarus Citibus
Provincial, Fareham	7	Dennis Dart/UVG Urban Star
Pullman, Swansea	2	Dennis Dart/Plaxton Pointer
Q Drive	10	Scania L113/Northern Counties
Quickstep, Leeds	4	Mercedes T2/Plaxton Beaver
R&I, London	2	Optare Metrorider
	4	Dennis Dart/Plaxton Pointer
	5	MAN 11.190/Optare Vecta
Ralph, Langley	3	Volvo B6LE/Wright Crusader
Reading Transport	3	DAF SB220/Optare Delta
	1	MAN 11.190/Optare Vecta
Redby, Sunderland	2	Volvo B6/Alexander Dash
	1	Volvo B10B/Alexander Strider
Rhondda	2	Mercedes O405/Optare Prisma
	3	Dennis Dart/Wright Handybus
	11	Mercedes T2/WS Coachbuilders
Richards, Cardigan	1	Dennis Dart/Plaxton Pointer
Rider York	20	Scania L113/Wright Axcess-ultralow
Sanders, Holt	1	DAF SB220/Ikarus Citibus
Sargeants, Kington	1	Mercedes O405/Optare Prisma
Selkent	52	Volvo Olympian/Northern Counties
Shamrock, Pontypridd	6	Dennis Dart/Northern Counties
	3	Dennis Dart/Marshall
Shaws, Chester-le-Street	6	Dennis Dart/Plaxton Pointer
Shearings	56	Volvo B10M/Van Hool
	30	Volvo B10M/Jonckheere Deauville
Sheffield Omnibus	8	Volvo B6/Alexander Dash
The Shires	33	Mercedes/Plaxton Beaver
	23	Scania L113/East Lancs
Simmons, Gonerby	1	Dennis Dart/Plaxton Pointer
Solent Blue Line	2	Volvo Olympian/East Lancs
	18	Iveco 59.12/Mellor
South London	12	Dennis Dart/Plaxton Pointer
South Wales Transport	17	Dennis Dart/Plaxton Pointer
Southampton Citybus	9	Dennis Dart/Plaxton Pointer
	1	Volvo B10B/Plaxton Verde
Southend Transport	4	Dennis Lance SLF/Wright Pathfinder
Southern National	6	Mercedes T2/Alexander Sprint
	4	Mercedes T2/Wright NimBus
Southern Vectis	8	Volvo Olympian/Northern Counties
Sovereign Bus & Coach	5	Volvo B10B/Wright Endurance
Sovereign (Harrow)	7	Mercedes T2/Plaxton Beaver
Speedlink Airport Services	30	Dennis Lance SLF/Berkhof
	7	DAF SB220/Northern Counties
	2	Dennis Dart/Northern Counties
Star Line, Knutsford	5	Mercedes T2/Alexander Sprint
	1	Dennis Dart/Northern Counties
	5	Scania L113/Wright/Axcess-ultralow (z)
Stewart, Inverinan	1	Dennis Dart/Plaxton Pointer
Stokes, Carstairs	2	Volvo B6/Alexander Dash
Strathclyde Buses	2	Volvo Olympian/Alexander Royale
	2	Volvo Olympian/Northern Counties
Strathtay Scottish	4	Volvo Olympian/Northern Counties
	2	Dennis Dart/Northern Counties
Stuart, Manchester	3	Dennis Dart/Plaxton Pointer
Tayside Transport	4	Volvo B6/Plaxton Pointer
Tees & District	25	Mercedes O405/Optare Prisma
Thames Transit	36	Dennis Dart/Plaxton Pointer
	6	Mercedes T2/Marshall
Thamesdown	9	Dennis Dart/Plaxton Pointer
Thamesway	28	Dennis Dart/Plaxton Pointer (z)
	19	Volvo B10M/Plaxton Premiere
TIBS, Singapore	50	Scania L113/Alexander Strider
	50	DAF SB220/Alexander Setanta
Timeline Travel	17	Dennis Javelin/Neoplan Transliner
	6	Volvo B6/Alexander Dash
	6	Volvo B10L/Alexander Ultra
Transmac, Macau	10	Dennis Dart/Plaxton Pointer
Trent	4	Mercedes T2/Wright NimBus
	15	Dennis Lance/Optare Sigma
	26	Optare MetroRider
Ulsterbus	60	Volvo B10L/Alexander Ultra (z)
Universitybus	2	Mercedes OH1416/Wright Urbanranger
	2	Dennis Dart/Wright Handybus
	4	Dennis Dart/Marshall
Wallace Arnold	35	Volvo B10M/Plaxton
Walls, Manchester	6	DAF DB250/Northern Counties
	2	DAF SB220/Ikarus
Warrington	7	Dennis Dart/Marshall
	4	Dennis Dart/Plaxton Pointer
Wealden Beeline	1	Dennis Dart/WS Coachbuilders
West Coast, Campbeltown	3	Optare MetroRider
West Midlands Travel	50	Volvo B10B/Wright Endeavour (z)
West Riding Group	7	Optare MetroRider
West Sussex CC	8	Blue Bird CS/Blue Bird
Western National	23	Dennis Dart/Plaxton Pointer
	1	Dennis Lance SLF/Wright Pathfinder
Westlink	8	MAN 11.190/Optare Vecta
White, Bridge of Walls	1	Scania L113/Wright
	1	Volvo B6/Wright Crusader
Whittle, Kidderminster	1	Dennis Dart/Northern Counties
Wigan Bus Company	1	DAF DB250/Northern Counties
	3	Dennis Dart/Northern Counties
Wilts & Dorset	12	DAF DB250/Optare Spectra
	4	Optare MetroRider
Yorkshire Coastliner	4	Volvo Olympian/Alexander Royale

Yorkshire Rider	50 Dennis Dart/Alexander Dash	Yorkshire Travel	6 Volvo B6/Alexander Dash
	68 Dennis Dart/Plaxton Pointer	Yorkshire Traction	5 Scania L113/East Lancs
	48 Dennis Lance/Plaxton Verde		3 Dennis Dart/Northern Counties
	63 Mercedes T2/Plaxton Beaver		1 Spartan/East Lancs Opus 2
Yorkshire Terrier	2 Volvo B6/Alexander Dash	Yorkshire Woollen	6 Mercedes T2/Plaxton Beaver
	6 Dennis Dart/Northern Counties		

Forward orders

Orders announced in 1995 for delivery in 1996

Bournemouth Transport	10 Dennis Dart/East Lancs	Ribble	6 Dennis Lance SLF/Berkhof
Brighton Transport	15 Dennis Dart SLF/Plaxton Pointer	Rossendale	4 Dennis Dart/East Lancs
Brighton & Hove	20 Dennis Lance/Optare Sigma	SB Holdings	150 Volvo Olympian/Alexander R
British Bus 1996-97	127 Dennis Dart SLF/Plaxton Pointer	Scania stock	10 Scania N113/East Lancs Cityzen
	97 Dennis Dart SLF/East Lancs	Shearings 1996	20 Volvo B10M/Van Hool
	73 Scania L113/East Lancs		15 Volvo B10M/Jonckheere
	65 Volvo Olympian/Northern Counties	Singapore Bus Services	200 Volvo Olympian
	45 Optare Metrorider		150 Volvo B10M
	71 Mercedes T2/Plaxton Beaver	Stagecoach	400 Mercedes T2/Alexander Sprint
	55 Mercedes T2/Alexander Sprint		140 Volvo Olympian/Northern Counties
Cambus	2 Optare MetroRider		100 Volvo Olympian/Alexander R
Capital Citybus	11 Volvo Olympian/Northern Counties		100 Dennis Dart/Alexander Dash
CMB, Hong Kong	20 Volvo Olympian		60 Volvo B10M/Plaxton Premiere
Derby City Transport	10 Mercedes T2/Alexander Sprint		60 Volvo B10M/Alexander PS
Dublin Bus	70 Volvo Olympian/Alexander R		10 Volvo B10M/Plaxton Expressliner
	10 Volvo B10B/Alexander		10 Volvo B10M artic/Plaxton Premier
Excelsior, Bournemouth	22 Volvo B10M/Plaxton		110 ERF Trailblazer
GM Buses North	5 Volvo B10L/Wright Liberator	Thamesdown	1 MAN 11.190/UVG Urban Star
Hong Kong Citybus	50 Volvo Olympian/Alexander R	Ulsterbus	34 Volvo B10M/Plaxton
KMB, Hong Kong	180 Volvo Olympian	Wallace Arnold	51 Volvo B10M/Plaxton Premiere
	2 Dennis Dart SLF/Plaxton Pointer	West Midlands Travel	100 Volvo B10L/Wright Liberator (b)
London & Country	13 Dennis Dart/East Lancs		
	15 Dennis Lance/East Lancs		
	10 Dennis Lance/East Lancs dd		
	4 Dennis Dominator/East Lancs		

a	delivered in 1994-95
b	originally ordered as B10Bs.
c	originally ordered as 7 Mercedes T2/Alexander Sprint
e	diverted from Midland Bluebird
z	delivered in 1995-96

London Central	21 Volvo Olympian/Northern Counties
Lothian	33 Volvo Olympian/Alexander Royale
Mainline	40 Volvo B10M/Alexander PS
Merseyside Transport	60 Volvo B10B/Wright Endurance
MTL London Northern	12 MAN 11.220/Marshall
Northumbria	12 Scania N113/East Lancs Cityzen
Preston Bus	12 Optare MetroRider
Redwing Coaches	14 Volvo B10M/Plaxton Premiere

Walls of Manchester bought its first new double-deckers in 1995. These were DAF DB250s with Northern Counties Palatine II bodies. *Stewart J Brown*